(Re)Discovering Charity

(Re)Discovering Charity

Andrew Lightbown
and
Nick Fane

First published in Great Britain in 2009

The University of Buckingham Press
Yeomanry House
Hunter Street
Buckingham MK18 1EG

A CIP catalogue record for this book is available at the British Library.

ISBN 978056043511

Andrew Lightbown worked in the investment management industry for fifteen years. Andrew first visited Kabubbu, with Quicken Trust, in 2004. His experience in Uganda and his friendship with the people of Quicken Trust led Andrew to radically review his vocation. Andrew left the City of London in 2006 and returned to university. Andrew now lectures in Management and Business Ethics at the University of Buckingham. His research is concerned with understanding the economic manifestations and consequences of Christian charity. Andrew is married to Sallyanne and they have two daughters: Katherine and Elizabeth. The Lightbown family regularly visit Kabubbu and are actively involved with the work and mission of Quicken Trust.

Nick Fane has been a teacher (of English), education officer and local government manager. Now formally retired from (but informed by experience in) these roles, he works part-time as a counsellor for a Christian counselling agency, among other voluntary activities. He has a long-standing amateur interest in the psychology of religion. He is married to Sue and they have a grown-up family. They are supporters of Quicken Trust's work in Uganda, and frequently visit South Africa.

In acknowledgement

Quicken Trust is delighted to have worked with the authors, Andrew Lightbown and Nick Fane, in producing this pamphlet. The pamphlet is the second in the Quickening Kabubbu series. When Andrew and Nick suggested to Quicken Trust a pamphlet that focused on explaining and illustrating the application of Christian charity we were only happy to endorse and sponsor such an approach. True charity is fundamental to the Christian way of life; it is also the underlying ethic, or virtue, which informs the work of Quicken Trust. Charity is both active and transformative. Quicken Trust is a charity in the legal sense of the term but, more importantly, it is the theological, rather than the legal definition, that inspires us in our daily activities. As a Christian charity Quicken Trust seeks to love those who it serves. However, an important part of our role is also to act as an intermediary between sympathetic donors and grateful recipients. When these two parties are brought together good really does grow at compound interest. It is a privilege to serve the people of Kabubbu and we can only do so because of the charity so freely given by our many donors. To our donors we say thank you.

We know that writing this pamphlet has been a labour of love for Andrew and Nick. They have written for a wide audience but the fruits of their work will flow, in the first instance, to Quicken Trust and the people of Kabubbu, for any royalties the authors may receive have been assigned to Quicken Trust. Andrew and Nick have been provided with help, guidance, and encouragement by countless others who have reviewed their work, asked probing questions, given up their family time, and made endless cups of tea whilst our authors have buried their heads in books and bashed way at their keyboards. Particular thanks must go to the academics who reviewed their work, some of whom have provided generous endorsements. Professor Jim Rafferty, from the University of Buckingham, critiqued and challenged some of the author's initial propositions. His insights were invaluable. Andrew and

Nick's friend Frank Hartley provided wise counsel, constant encouragement and theological rigour. Sallyanne Lightbown and Sue Fane have provided consistent encouragement, endless patience and honest appraisal. To all of who have been involved in this project we can only express our gratitude. *Agape*.

Geoff and Geraldine Booker. Cowbeech, September 2009.

Finally, this pamphlet was written at a very difficult time in the family life of one of its authors and although we hope that the finished work will stimulate both thought and action we are happy that this work has been produced, in part, in loving memory of:

Allan Roy Morgan 1935-2009, a generous, kind and loving man.

Quicken Trust is a U.K. registered charity. The sole purpose of Quicken Trust is to assist the people of Kabubbu in their journey towards sustainability. Quicken Trust was first invited to Kabubbu, a village twenty miles north of the capital of Uganda, in 1999. Despite being so close to Kampala the locals describe the area as the jungle: they described themselves as the forgotten people. They had no water, no medical care and no work other than quarrying and subsistence farming. They lived in poverty and dejection. For decades the forgotten people had suffered dreadfully at the hands of the three big diseases that have affected much of Sub Saharan Africa: political tyranny, Malaria and HIV AIDS. For the last ten years Quicken Trust has been telling the story of the forgotten people of Kabubbu in the U.K. Ordinary people, acting either as individuals or on behalf of organisations they represent, have responded charitably to the stories that have been told. Without charity the people of Kabubbu would still be forgotten, living in dejection and without hope, unable to educate their children or look after their sick. Kabubbu and its citizens are no longer forgotten.
You can learn more about Quicken Trust through its website: www.quickentrust.com

Contents

Writing this pamphlet has been a voyage of discovery for its authors. For a long while we have both been aware that Christianity has only three theological virtues and the one that will endure, it is said by Christianity's first theologian, St. Paul, is charity. The other two virtues are faith and hope. Charity is central to the Christian way of life. Indeed a stained glass window in the authors' church reminds Christians of the requirement to become *rooted in charity*. Despite charity's central role in Christianity it is under attack from business leaders, development economists, politicians and countless others who regularly proclaim its impotence. Indeed charity is considered by many to lead already vulnerable people into a state of increased dependency. If Christian charity is a poor substitute for modern day political and economically inspired secular approaches, then one of the most basic tenets of Christianity is called into doubt and Paul's anthem to *agape*[1] can be considered as superficial, albeit beautifully crafted, poetry.

If charity is indeed impotent then Jesus' answer to the question *'What does it mean to love my neighbour?'* is redundant. For in answer to that question we are given the Parable of the Samaritan, the telling of which shows Christian charity in action. Our experience leads us to suggest that real charity, Christian charity, in fact leads to commitment, responsibility and well-being (economic, psychological and spiritual) and that the reason the critics attack charity is that they have failed to understand its real meaning. Charity needs rediscovering because it works. The consequence of charity, willingly given and gratefully accepted, is that the immediate recipient in turn becomes a charitable giver. Why? Because responsibility and hope appear to be the natural consequences of the *seemingly* unnatural love we refer to as charity. In attempting to rediscover charity we do not claim to have cracked the code, nor do we assert that the exercise of true charity is the sole preserve of those who identify themselves as Christians. Also, we do not claim to understand the ideal of Christian charity fully: we probably

---

[1] New Testament 1 Corinthians Chapter 13

never will, for Christian charity is the most demanding form of love, and perhaps all we are capable of is to *'see through a glass, darkly'*.[2]

This pamphlet has three sections. In the first, we seek to explore the defining characteristics of Christian charity, drawing mainly on academic literature. In the second, we reproduce and illustrate one of the most famous stories ever told. And in the final section we tell the stories of sixteen recipients of gift love (charity) whom we were privileged to interview in the Ugandan village of Kabubbu, in June 2009.[3] Kabubbu is a small village (population circa 4,200) 13 miles to the north of Kampala in the Republic of Uganda. In common with many African villages it has been afflicted with Africa's three big diseases, malaria, political tyranny and HIV. The nature of the gifts they received fall into four categories: houses, income-producing assets, HIV treatment, counselling/prayer.

To all of those who welcomed us into their homes and shared their stories with us, we say thank you. All willingly gave permission to tell them to you, and although the ethical standards we have adopted have mandated us to change some names and details, to ensure privacy and safety, their words are always their own.

This pamphlet aims to assist in the process of (re)discovering charity. The prefix has deliberately been placed in brackets as a visual acknowledgement that our knowledge remains incomplete. We are committed to continuing research into the properties and manifestations of Christian charity and will in time consider the role of donors and charities themselves. We are however convinced of three things. First, that Christian charity is misunderstood and frequently confused with aid. Secondly, that Christian charity is a force for good and, thirdly, that it is underemployed.

Andrew Lightbown and Nick Fane, August 2009.

---

[2] 1 Corinthians 13 and 12.

[3] It should be noted that the visit in June 2009 was the third such visit and in all over forty interviews have been held in Kabubbu with recipients of charitable giving.

SECTION 1

Either: '*We need to recover an older tradition – essentially a set of religious traditions – that spoke of human solidarity, of justice and compassion, and of the non-negotiable dignity of individual lives.*'
Rabbi Jonathan Sacks

Or: '*The weak and ill-constituted shall perish: first principle of our philanthropy. And one shall help them to do so. What is more harmful than any vice, active sympathy for the ill-constituted and weak – Christianity.*'
Nietzsche

Introduction

This offering is the result of three different promptings. First, experience: we were aware that the application of Christian charity does indeed transform lives and not simply those of the immediate recipient. Secondly, our own personal faith. Thirdly, literature: the literature we refer to is mostly academic and although we hope that academics will take our work seriously we wish to stimulate wider thought and reflection.

It is important to stress that our approach to understanding charity began, in fact, with grounded experience, informed by the stories we were told in Kabubbu. Our approach was then refined through reflection and study.

Of the thinkers who guided our thought process and challenged our preconceived ideas one of the most significant has been C.S. Lewis. Lewis, although not a classically trained theologian, was one of the deepest Christian thinkers of the twentieth century. His novels and stories caught the attention of successive generations.

Lewis provided us with two specific insights which intrigued us and seemed to support what we already knew from experience.

In 'Mere Christianity' Lewis[4] wrote that 'both good and evil grow at compound interest.' The stories that we tell in the second half of this book demonstrate that Lewis was correct: charity which is a good, or in theological terms a virtue, does indeed have a compounding effect. The fact that charity is a good is important because, as we shall see in the next section, charity is an antidote to bad, evil, or a state of ill-being. From an economic pers-pective, Christian charity is a good or an asset, which promotes, and frequently secures, well-being. Lewis also reminds us that for the Christian,

---

[4] Lewis C.S. (2002). *Mere Christianity 50th Anniversary Edition.* London U.K. Harper Collins.

charity is part of our basic morality. Christianity has only three theological virtues: faith, hope and charity. And as Paul reminds us in 1 Corinthians 13 v. 13, charity is the virtue that endures. Paul's letter was specifically to and for the people of Corinth; however, his theological insights have become widely accepted as universal truths by the majority of Christians, although, as we shall see, faith, hope and charity remain inextricably joined. It appears that hope and charity, in particular, are properties and manifestations of each other.

In the King James Version of the Bible verse we read: *'And now abideth faith, hope, charity, these three; but the greatest of these is charity.'*[5] It is well worth reading this famous passage in the King James Version and comparing the response experienced with a more contemporary translation where the word 'love' is used instead of 'charity'. For the Christian reader it is interesting to note that 'love' and 'charity' can often be used interchangeably, as they are translations of the Greek word *'agape'*. So, if we are to understand and quicken our sense of charity we need to understand *agape* and, in particular, how *agape* differs from other forms of love.

Agape is the form of love most commonly referred to in the New Testament and it does differ from other forms of love. When Jesus summed up the two commandments and when the expert in the law asked Jesus to clarify what it means to love our neighbour as ourselves, the love referred to was *agape*. When Paul talks of faith, hope and charity, the charity that he espouses is synonymous with *agape*. Both Jesus and Paul had a profound understanding that Christian love, or Christian charity, grows at compound interest. And the charity or love they refer to is *agape*. *Agape* is a notoriously hard concept to define. The definition that we use in this pamphlet has been taken from Thomas Jay Oord and is: *'to act intentionally, in sympathetic response to others (including God) to promote well-being.*[6]

---

[5] 1 Corinthians 13:13.

[6] Oord T.J. (2005) The Love Racket: Defining Love and Agape for the Love-and-Science Research Programme. *Zygon,* Vol. 40, No. 4, Dec. p 919. Authors' emphasis.

Lewis also provides Christians and others with a direct challenge, for he suggests that when we fail to engage with charity, or as he sometimes calls it 'gift-love', we are failing to accept the most significant part of a moral code that comprises the Christian way of life. The Christian's response to ill-being must be, first, a spiritual and not a political response. This does not, of course, mean that the Christian should not have political views or that the Christian should not be politically active. But it does mean that the Christian is first and foremost called on to live out his or her faith in a manner that is both practical and loving. Practicality and spirituality are not, we suggest, polar opposites. For some, spirituality may be a call to poverty, prayer and silence; for others, spirituality may occur in our response to life's encounters. The exercise of Christian spirituality may be contingent on a) our own personal sense of calling and b) the starting point for our spiritual journey. Wherever we start from, however, the Christian is also called on to become involved and, therefore, accountable. Matthew 26, where Jesus narrates the Last Judgement (the Parable of the Sheep and the Goats), should serve as a sharp reminder to Christians of the importance of personal involvement in charity, *agape* or love.

Indeed the Gospels are full of such sentiments. When Jesus speaks, it is not about (other than to condemn it) religiosity. It is about feeding the hungry and caring for the sick, whoever they are, wherever they come from, and whatever they have done. It is at the heart of what Jesus means by 'I am the way', and is a message given so clearly and so repeatedly that it cannot be ignored (though it often is).

The Christian needs to be especially careful not to look initially for solutions that are explicitly political, or to subcontract their giving through the mechanism of the ballot box. For a Christian it is their sense of spirituality and theology which informs their political and economic orientation, and not the other way round. The exercise of Christian charity should not be subject to the limits of political techniques. Christians need, through personal example, to show how charity is profoundly different in application and consequence to politicised, secular responses which frequently masquerade as charity, or gift love - the most obvious example being aid. Lewis's challenge to us (it is worth remembering that he was writing over fifty years ago) is worth reflecting on as a not-so-gentle reminder of our most basic obligations. This is what Lewis wrote:

> *'Some people nowadays say that charity ought to be unnecessary and that instead of giving to the poor we ought to be producing a society in which there were no poor to give to. They might be quite right in saying that we ought to produce this kind of society. But if anyone thinks that, as a consequence, you can stop giving in the meantime, then he has parted company with Christian morality.'*[7]

Lewis, we suggest, is right and the stories in the third section of this pamphlet give many practical instances that show that Lewis was also correct when he suggested that good has that incredible compounding effect.

It is important that Christians, and others, rediscover and promote charity because charity is under attack. It is under attack for two reasons. First, it is a spiritual good and will therefore always be attacked by spiritual bads (outright acts of evil, false prophets etc.) Secondly, it is misunderstood. Christian charity, as we shall see in the coming section, is not the same as aid, philanthropy or even altruism. It is more profound, more specific, less instinctive and further reaching. In writing this pamphlet we make frequent reference to Anders Nygren. Nygren suggests that spontaneity is a characteristic of *agape*. We are not so sure that this is universally true. In the ideal, or theoretical world, a spontaneous response may well occur, as indeed it did in the Parable of the Samaritan. Grounded research[8] suggests that there is frequently a gap between seeing or experiencing ill-being and taking affirmative, long-term and committed action. Spontaneity may of

---

[7] Lewis C.S. (2002). *Mere Christianity 50th anniversary edition.* London U.K. Harper Collins. p 86.

[8] Rima: as yet unpublished PhD.

course occur in certain situations or be a defining concept of what we might think of as 'ideal *agape*.' Reliance on free will and intentionality frequently gives rise to what we might think of as (Lightbown and Fane) 'realised *agape*.'

Christian charity is a form of spiritual economy. It is an activity through which we can, to borrow a phrase from Kathy Galloway, 'share the blessing'. When we share the blessing, a miracle frequently occurs, the blessing grows. We provide practical illustrations of this in the third part of the book and for those seeking a biblical imperative we suggest a re-reading of the Feeding of the Five Thousand. As a point of interest it is worth noting that the boy who gave the gifts of fish and bread remained anonymous. Anonymity is frequently a characteristic of *agape*. Ridley asks 'How many people do you know who are true altruists?'[9] He answers his own question with the answer *'Very, very few.'* His answer seems highly plausible, though not necessarily for the reasons he provides, for anonymity and humility may well be dominant characteristics of truly selfless giving.

---

[9] Ridley M. (1997). *The Origins of Virtue.* U.K. Penguin. p 21.

Chapter 1:
Quickening Charity

'This is how we know what love is: Jesus Christ laid down his life for us. And we ought to lay down our lives for our brothers. If anyone has material possessions and sees his brother in need but has no pity on him, how can the love of God be in him?'[10]

To quicken is a Middle English word meaning to breathe new life into, or to restore to life. It is a word laden with meaning for the Christian faith. The Book of Common Prayer, for instance, refers to the 'quick and the dead.' Quicken Trust works alongside the people of Kabubbu in the quickening of their community. The source of much of the gift-love, or charity, is ordinary households in the U.K. Future research will focus on the donor 'community', who we hypothesise act out of sympathy, with sympathy being a property of love, to quicken the well being of others. Proponents of selfish gene theory, starting with Williams and Hamilton in the mid 1960s, have tended to take the view that when:

> *'a modern biologist seeing an animal doing something to benefit another assumes either that it is being manipulated by the other or that it is being subtly selfish.'*[11]

We do not seek to criticise selfish gene theory (after all, the idea that mankind may be inherently selfish would hardly be a revelation to students of either theology or history) but we do suggest that exercise of Christian charity shows that we are capable of acting in a manner that is in fact entirely unselfish.

We believe that the notion of charity, in its specifically Christian context, requires quickening, starting with a re-defining, indeed a re-discovery, of

---

[10] 1 John 3 16-18 New International Version.
[11] Op. cit. Ridley. p 18.

charity. In recent years charity has acquired in secular circles something of a bad name. Proclamations such as *'Charity creates dependency'*, *'Charity patronises the receiver'*, *'Charity disappears through deliberate corruption or inefficient administration'* are made by the sceptical and the cynical, who seldom offer hard empirical evidence, perhaps because they are referring to something other than Christian charity.

We believe that these are misconceptions, based on a distorted understanding of what proper charity is, and confusion with the modern notion of aid. If the true nature of charity, as implied by St Paul in his use of the Greek word *agape,* and as subsequently developed by generations of Christian thinkers, can be rediscovered, its wholly beneficial effect will become evident. The exercise of true Christian charity is marked by effectiveness and reverence. The manifestations of charity appear to be: 1) hope; 2) increased material and spiritual well-being; and 3) a heightened sense of virtue in the recipient leading to an increased sense of responsibility towards the a) donor and b) their immediate neighbours (community).

We argue that *agape* charity is clearly different from some related concepts. For example, it is not altruism, which is often done for the benefit of the giver, or at least the gene pool. Nor is it aid, which is often ideologically or politically motivated. It is not even love, in the erotic and devotional sense or even in the sense of liking. Christian charity also differs from modern secular and political definitions of charity, with their focus on public interest, and from philanthropy, which seeks to foster general or communal well-being. We are not making the case that secular charity and philanthropy are poor substitutes for Christian charity, merely that they are different. Philanthropy, according to Brentlinger,[12] can be regarded as the giving (of money) out of a love for mankind in general and sympathy for some of the conditions that affect large sections of the population, such as HIV or illiteracy, but in situations where the giver does not enter into a long-term and committed

---

[12] Cited in Soble A. (1989). *Eros, Agape and Philia-Readings in the Philosophy of Love.* New York U.S.A. Paragon House.

relationship with an individual recipient. Such philanthropy often feeds, and works through, charity and charities. Christian charity, by contrast, is direct, personal and characterised by long-term commitment. Both philanthropy and Christian charity may derive from faith and Christian morality.

Modern translations of the Bible use 'love' as their translation of the Greek word *'agape'*, though so did William Tyndale 1526. The Revised Version of the Bible (1881) was the first mass-produced translation to use 'love' throughout, whereas the Wycliffe c 1380 and King James versions (1611) refer to charity. It is therefore mainly from the late Victorian era onwards that 'charity' has all but disappeared from common use in this sense. However, Christian charity remains a specifically theological virtue and should not be confused with modern secular definitions of charity, which focus on issues such as public interest and activities in the 'third sector.'

Replacing 'charity' with 'love' may be regarded as just a matter of semantics, but the consequences may be more far reaching than intended. There is a danger that unless the nature of the love referred to is recognised there is a shift in meaning, and something with a hard ethical edge becomes solely emotionally based, diluted and sentimentalised in the process. Christian charity, as described by Phillips and Taylor[13], 'functioned as a cultural element, binding individuals into society' until it came 'under increasing attack from competitive individualism.' Competitive economic individualism and the search for top down political solutions both appear to be part of an historical trend that has served to undermine individual responsibility and Christian charity.

When the New Testament refers to love it is also most frequently a direct translation of *agape*. The theologian Colin Grant says that:

> *'according to Young's Analytical Concordance, the word agape occurs one hundred and fifteen times in the New Testament, philia itself*

---

[13] Phillips K. and Taylor B. (2009). *On Kindness.* London U.K. Hamish Hamilton. p 5.

occurs only eighteen times and compounds like philadelphia and philanthropia, sixteen times, for a total of thirty-four occurrences of all variations of the word philia.'[14]

Agape, or charity, is therefore a specific type of love, and if we are to quicken or redefine charity we must reach an understanding of how *agape* is radically different from other and more natural loves. For when we are commanded to love our neighbour as ourselves we are also being told to love in a way that supersedes natural affection, genetic programming, cultural norms and friendship. *Agape* and Christian charity also refute self-regard and the requirement for recognition. When we engage in acts of charity we are reaching beyond that which is normal, comfortable and natural. We are able to do so because of the freedom to choose with which we have been blessed. Thomas Oord describes the importance of freedom succinctly when he suggests that:

> *'love is meaningless if individuals are not free to choose one action rather than others.'* [15]

The intentional and loving deployment of free will is the answer to the biologist George Williams' question

> *'How could maximizing selfishness produce an organism capable of advocating, and occasionally practising,* **charity** *towards strangers and even animals?'*[16]

Free will and charity, it seems, are bound together. Paradoxically, however, as Christians and philosophers (Kant for example) have discovered, free will frequently leads to the voluntary adoption of long-term duty and obligation to others.

---

[14] Grant C. For Love of God. *Journal of Religious,* Volume 24, Issue 1, spring 1996, p 8.

[15] Oord 2005: p 925.

[16] Ridley 1997:p 35. Authors' emphasis.

It is in viewing Jesus' mandate (to love our neighbour) as a duty and an obligation that we begin to understand why it is in fact a commandment, rather than a suggestion or piece of well intentioned advice. The adoption of such agapeistic attitudes may, on occasion, lead to impoverishment but, perhaps most frequently, to an altered attitude towards the material world and possessions. The call to absolute poverty is one of discernment and should clearly not be entered into lightly. The commandment to give, however, forms part of everyday Christian morality. A calling to poverty is personal; the command to give charitably would seem to be universal.

The Samaritan made a choice to offer charity, or *agape*, to a neighbour who could not be defined by friendship, cultural equivalence, family ties or shared interests. The Parable of the Samaritan completely, utterly and in the most shocking way redefines the whole concept of the neighbour, and if it is to the neighbour that we must address our love, charity, or *agape* then those words were quickened through the telling of one short story. The parable, according to theologians Anders Nygren and Richard Foster, is a statement of transvaluation whereby the concept of love is revolutionised. This does not imply that we should not love those nearest and dearest and that our love cannot be giving and kind - but it does suggest that such natural loves, addressed to the near neighbour, require different terminology.

Lewis refers to these more natural forms of love as affection/*storge* (fondness through familiarity – love to our family and near neighbours), friendship/*philia* (bonds created through a common or shared interest – hence philanthropy being a gift directed towards a shared interest or a communal benefit - and therefore frequently characterised by reciprocity and mutuality) and *eros* (devotional and exclusive love). The philosopher and theologian Søren Kierkegaard, in Works of Love (1872), as quoted by Outka, in differentiating *agape* wrote:

> '*Erotic love is determined by the object; friendship is determined by the object; only love to one's neighbour is determined by love. Since*

ones' neighbour is unconditionally everyman, all distinctions are removed from the object.' [17]

That is to say that all distinctions are removed because all men are held to be created with inherent value. Charity is a process, perhaps the process through which value is created, for as Kierkegaard also comments:

'Your neighbour is everyman, for on the basis of distinctions he is not your neighbour, nor on the basis of likeness to you as being different from other men. He is your neighbour on the basis of equality with you before God; but this equality absolutely every man has, and he has it absolutely.' [18]

The Parable of the Samaritan and the concept of *agape* both suggest that whilst charity may begin at home it certainly extends beyond one's immediate context and environment. Biologists and social scientists often struggle with the concepts such as true altruism and charity which they regard as non genetic (biologists) and economically irrational (social scientists). Dawkins, for instance, has written about humans being gene-tically selfish. He may well be right and Christians should not necessarily worry about scientific explanation: after all the concept of original sin, which specifically refers to man's inherent selfishness, somewhat predates genetic discovery. Selfishness may be regarded as a source of ill being: Christian charity as we shall see counters ill being. As we shall see, although sharing common properties, true altruism and charity are in essence subtly different.

Altruism is a particularly slippery concept, existing as it does in different forms, as Polkinghorne and Beale, both scientists and Christians, point out when they argue that:

---

[17] Cited in Outka G. (1972). *Agape and Ethical Analysis.* New Haven U.S.A. Yale University Press. p 1.

[18] ibid: p 159.

> *'true altruism exceeds kin altruism (within the family gene pool) or reciprocal altruism (helping another in expectation of return). When someone risks his life in order to save an unknown and unrelated child from a burning building, there is an altruism of an order that exceeds evolutionary explanation.'*

They go on to point out that:

> *'although a great deal is now understood about the conditions under which 'altruistic' behaviour will evolve in populations, it is neither a substitute for ethics, nor does it explain ethics away... After all, 'take up your cross' is hardly an invitation to worldly success.'*[19]

This suggests that 'true' altruism appears to be spontaneous, and in the example the altruistic response is to promote greater well-being, in response to perceived danger/ill-being. Charity/*agape* appears by contrast to be more deliberate, intentional and a matter of will. Altruism may be a short term and immediate response; for example, we hope we don't have to save the boy from the burning building more than once. Charity by contrast as shown in the Kabubbu stories is a long-term commitment. Both charity and true altruism can be seen as virtuous because they both regard all human life as sacred, worthwhile. Polkinghorne's statement about ethics perhaps brings out this distinction - that is to say ethics is concerned with dilemma, judgment and choice. Ethics, and Christian ethics in our case, therefore suggest that humans are capable of acting in a way that supersedes natural, or genetic, predisposition. Perhaps whilst acts of altruism show humans at their evolved and spontaneous best, acts of *agape* depict humans at their intentional best. The term altruism can also be used to refer to a general and generous principle of living, whilst charity is about generosity as demonstrated through specific and intentional action. As stated earlier, Anders Nygren took the view that *agape* is spontaneous, whereas we suggest that 'realised *agape*' is often deliberate and intentional.

---

[19] Polkinghorne J. and Beale N. (2009). *Questions of Truth*. U.K. Westminster John Knox Press. p 144.

A distinction between true altruism and Christian charity may not be quite as clear as even we would like to make it. We have offered some points for reflection in the paragraph above. However, the Shorter Oxford English Dictionary reveals that the term altruism was brought into use in English in the mid nineteenth century by secular philosophers such as John Stuart Mill and Auguste Comte and began to replace charity, particularly in those intellectual circles who were becoming antagonistic to religion and who needed a new word to fit their world view. The deepest question could now be conveniently avoided! This caused Frederick Farrar to wonder whether (Oxford English Dictionary) 'altruism is a sweeter word than charity.' In our attempt to rediscover charity, we hope to reclaim the word and reinstate it in its former place in discussions of ethics and morality. Altruism may be the sweeter word, for those who like their drink artificially sweetened!

This example of 'newspeak' has had something of the same effect that Schumacher[20] refers to when he observes how the thought police of Soviet Russia removed the churches from the street map of Leningrad, even though the 'living churches' remained. The widespread adoption of altruism, as an alternative term, has consigned Christian charity to the museum of theological relics.

Trying to understand our highest nature (or the supranatural) through the eyes of the natural is a strange approach in any case. Christian theology holds that two blessings combine to allow humans to offer such love-grace and free will. The exercise of free will is a choice that moves humans towards their highest potential. Free will allows humans to make the choice to act in a seemingly irrational manner. Outka[21] points out that in *agape* an individual first of all has to become 'self moving,' acting 'upon himself.' Acting upon oneself in this way moves one, always, in the direction of the other. Action in the first instance may feel unnatural.

---

[20] Schumacher E. (1977). *A Guide for the Perplexed*. U.K. Sphere Books. p 1.
[21] Outka 1972: p 129.

C.S. Lewis frequently refers to the importance of will, as in this quotation from The Four Loves:

> *'When He planted the garden of our nature and caused the flowering, fruiting loves to grow there He set our will to dress them... While we hack and prune we know very well that what we are hacking and pruning is big with a splendour and vitality which our rational will could never of itself have supplied. To liberate that splendour, to let it become fully what it is trying to be, to have all trees instead of scrubby tangles, and sweet apples instead of crabs, is part of our purpose.'*[22]

Outka draws upon Karl Barth, one of the twentieth century's most respected theologians, in stating that:

> *'faith and agape are not properties of human nature but definitive actions occurring to certain men.'*[23]

The point is surely this: we can choose to become one of those certain men - just as the Samaritan and countless others have done. Even Richard Dawkins concludes his account of The Selfish Gene by stating: *'We, alone on earth, can rebel against the tyranny of the selfish replicators.'* Lewis, Nygren and many other theologians might call this free will.

If engaging in Christian charity is in part a biologically unnatural task (in the sense of being above or beyond genetic or behavioural programming) it can also be considered as being irrational. And it is in the lack of rationality that Christian charity stands in contrast to secular and political responses. It stands in contrast because it is underpinned by a very important ethic, or spiritual value, which is seldom referred to in the secular political and economic realms. The ethic to which we are referring is reverence (regarding

---

[22] Lewis C.S (2002). *The Four Loves, Signature Classics Edition.* London U.K. Harper Collins. p 142, 143.
[23] Cited in Outka 1972: p 62.

each individual as uniquely different, and where difference is respected and encouraged) and, in particular, reverence towards the vulnerable. One of the biggest criticisms of charity is that it tends to dominate, imprison or colonise the other: in other words a state of dependency is said to be created. True Christian charity does not create dependency; instead it liberates and creates well-being. Perhaps such vulnerability was what Yeats had in mind when he wrote in He Wishes for the Cloths of Heaven:

> *'But I, being poor, have only my dreams; / I have spread my dreams under your feet; / Tread softly because you tread on my dreams.'*

Christian charity treads softly because it is underpinned by reverence. According to H. Richard Niebuhr, as quoted in Outka:

> *'Love is reverence; it keeps its distance even as it draws near; it does not seek to absorb the other in the self or want to be absorbed by it; it rejoices in the otherness of the other; it desires the beloved to be what he is and does not seek to refashion him into a replica of the self or to make him a means of the self's advancement.'*[24]

Reverence is the spiritual ethic that differentiates charity from aid or mere giving. To be reverent is, in the lexicon of contemporary economics, to act irrationally, for it seeks to give absolute priority to the interests of the beloved other. And, as Nygren suggests, when we place *agape*:

> *'in the context of ordinary human life it will always be seen as more or less of a paradox.'*[25]

Aid, by contrast, frequently gives priority to the interests of the donor. Aid is frequently given with conditions attached: true charity is by contrast unconditional. To act unconditionally is an anathema to modern, rationally

---

[24] Cited in Outka 1972: p 2.

[25] Nygren A. (1953). *Agape and Eros (translated by Phillip S. Watson, in 1969).* New York U.S.A. Harper Torchbooks. p 82.

inclined social sciences. It is perhaps a matter of shame that rational decisions are regarded as decisions that promote or protect self-interest as a first order priority. As Terry Eagleton says:

'Reason itself has been debased to mere self-interested calculation.'[26]

For Nygren, *agape* or Christian charity, is:

'directly opposed to all rational computation and calculation.'[27]

The point we make is this: that rational calculus and financial models cannot be used as a guide for charitable action (and some may be beginning to doubt their reliability in secular economy), but that the impact of charity can, in fact, be tracked and its value appreciated.

Colin Grant has stressed that:

'agape is a theocentric term that designates unqualified, radically self giving love...the term is not a rational, anthropocentric term...ethical categories such as concern about fairness and claims of self in relation to others do not apply.'[28]

Acting charitably frequently promotes justice and fairness although this is not its primary aim, for as we have seen in our preferred definition, increased well-being is the desired consequence of Christian charity. As a result of economic growth, giving in the developed world is most frequently undertaken by those who possess economic surplus. Scripture shows us, however, that even the poorest can be givers. In the account of the widow's mite Jesus tells the story of a woman who gave out of her deep poverty. The widow belonged to one of the two categories that should, according to

---

[26] Eagleton T. (2007). *The Meaning of Life.* Oxford U.K. Oxford University Press. p 22.

[27] Nygren op cit p 90.

[28] Grant C. For Love of God. *Journal of Religious,* Volume 24, Issue 1, Spring 1996. p 131.

James, have been a direct recipient of charity. Indeed in his epistle James defines the exercise of Christian religion partly in terms of such giving:

> *'Pure religion and undefiled before God and the Father is this, to visit the fatherless and widows in their affliction, and to keep oneself unspotted from the world.'[29]*

The parable of the widow's mite is an interesting challenge to those of us who do in fact enjoy economic surplus.

In many cases, such as the boy with five loaves and two fish, the surplus might be incredibly small. Stories from scripture stand contrary to views offered by academics such as Bonner who suggests that:

> *'Qur'anic notions of the purification and circulation of property illustrate a distinctly Islamic way of conceptualising charity, generosity, and poverty, markedly different from the Christian notion of perennial reciprocity between rich and poor and the ideal of charity as an expression of communal love.'[30]*

Whatever the critics such as Bonner state, *agape* and charity are in fact fundamental motifs of Christianity. Community is also clearly an important motif of Christianity but the experience we gained in Kabubbu and theological reflections both demonstrate that community frequently fails to embrace the diseased and destitute. When acting in *agape*, we act as neighbours, and are frequently required to do so when the immediate community (or family unit) fails to offer necessary love and support. Charity it seems is often called upon when the more natural loves (*storge* and *philia*) are absent. *Agape* in many ways for beneficiaries is the love of last resort. True Christian charity pays heed to Eleanor Roosevelt's advice that *'the most important thing in any relationship is not what you get but what you give,'*

---

[29] New Testament James 1 verse 27.

[30] Bonner M. Poverty and Economics in the Qur'an. *Journal of Interdisciplinary History,* xxxv:3, Winter 2005. p 392.

and as we have seen yet another paradox within the economy of charity is that it is often those with the least apparent surplus (the boy with his loaves and fish) who selflessly give. Charity may in many cases in fact represent a Christian notion of perennial giving to the poor, by the poor.

Grant's insight is particularly useful in that it reminds Christians that our guide is theology and faith, and that this does not need to be validated by reference to the natural, social or political sciences. Faith and theology, by contrast, should shape our understanding of subjects such as economics; for charity is, in part, an economic activity. Charity, or *agape*, is unashamedly an act of investment. A charitable investment strategy appears at first sight to be high risk, speculative and perhaps imprudent, but, as the stories in the second part of this pamphlet demonstrate, the pattern of returns, or the value that is created when an act of charity takes place, produce significant positive returns (materially, socially and spiritually).

So far we have described some of the characteristics of Christian charity and explained that charity is an act of gift-love, and that charity is a translation of the Greek *agape*. We now provide some specific definitions of *agape*. Using these definitions we will then describe why Christian charity is, in part, economic.

Avery Cardinal Dulles says that:

> *'agape impels us to pass onto others what we have received...when our gift-love is so graced that it goes out to include persons who are naturally unattractive and unlovable it deserves to be called charity in this theological sense of the word.'*[31]

The important point here is that charity is not something that should be extended solely towards vulnerable members of our own 'in group'. The fact

---

[31] Dulles A. Love, the Pope and C.S. Lewis. *Monthly Journal of Religion and Public Life,* Issue 169, January 2007. p 20, 24.

that sometimes we feel others to be unattractive or unlovable may, in reality, say more about us than we might care to admit. The Parable of the Samaritan reminds us that Christian charity should be offered to those with whom we have little natural affinity alongside the love we offer to those closer to home.

Charlene Burns believes:

> *'agape is not a thing to be sought; it is action, a way of being in the world that manifests the divine. Agape protects trusts, hopes and perseveres with the other in patience, kindness, selflessness, humility, equanimity, forgiveness.'[32]*

Ideal *agape* fulfils Christ's command 'to love others as I have loved you.'

For Richard Watts *'agape is the highest form of love and is primarily volitional and self giving rather than emotional and self centred.'[33]*

From these quotations we can see that Christian charity involves the flow of goods, or assets, always spiritual and most frequently material or financial. The flow of spiritual and material assets takes the form of a gift, but a gift given in reverence to the position of the other person as a uniquely created human being. The gift is literally given. Reciprocity is not a requirement. The Samaritan may, according to Outka, have hoped that a friendship (*storge*/affection) might develop but he certainly did not expect it, or make his act of charity contingent on some form of ongoing relationship or even recognition. The Samaritan gave entirely of himself using a variety of resources, specifically sympathy (a spiritual resource and always a component of *agape*), money and time. Sympathy leading to the giving of

---

[32] Burns P.E. Altruism In Nature As Manifestation Of Divine Energeia, *Zygon,* Volume 41, No.1. March 2006. p 131.

[33] Watts R. E. Biblical *Agape* as a Model of Social Interest. *Individual Psychology,* Volume 48, Number 1, March 1992. p 35.

material assets (financial or otherwise), and the spending of time with and for another human being, are all surely characteristic manifestations of a much-overused word, commitment. Commitment, we believe, is a necessary pre condition of responsibility. The Samaritan may have been more aware than many professionally trained theologians and academics from other disciplines, in his own and modern times, that he was required to live and love in a fashion that transcends bi-lateral relationships, where the guiding ethic can be summarised as 'you scratch my back and I'll scratch yours.' Depressingly frequently, some theologians seem compelled to defend reciprocity and mutuality as a basis for action. Kierkegaard's observation that:

> 'The Lover, who forgets himself, is remembered by love: there is one who thinks of him, and in this way it comes about that the lover gets what he gives.'[34]

reminds us that the cosmos does not necessarily operate on the basis of bilateral relationship.

Some Christians may be tempted to answer: 'Yes, but the commandment also tells me to love myself: in fact it tells me to love my neighbour as myself. Surely this means that my needs are at least equal to those of the other person.' This is a difficult debate and we don't pretend to know the answer to this question. However, we found Paul Ramsey's insights intriguing as an impetus for reflection. Ramsey poses the question:

'How exactly do you love yourself?' He then muses:

> 'answer this and you will know how a Christian should love his neighbour. You naturally love yourself for your own sake. You wish for your own good, and do so even though you have certain distaste for the kind of person you are. Liking yourself or thinking yourself very nice, or not, has fundamentally nothing to do with the matter. After a

---

[34] Cited in Outka 1972: p 67.

failure of some sort, the will to live soon returns and you always hold expectantly onto another possibility of attaining some good for yourself.'[35]

If we have hope for ourselves as, Ramsey implies, we ought to be concerned with the fulfilment of hope in others and one way that we can do this is by acting in *agape*.

In other words, if we love ourselves, in spite of our shortcomings and differences, we really ought to love others in the same way. If we are hopeful that others will accept and assist us when we know that they might find us less than loveable, then we ought to offer the same love. This is the only way that the Golden Rule, do unto others as you would have done unto you, can be fulfilled.

Brian Thorne has commented:

> *'To love one's neighbour as oneself is a hard commandment... for love of neighbour is in proportion to love of self.'[36]*

And, as our interviews demonstrate, loving oneself is made no easier by the guilts and anxieties associated (however mistakenly) with HIV infection and of trying to be a good parent when you have been abandoned by your partner and are unable to provide your children with sufficient food. The receipt of true Christian charity, we argue, creates and builds up stocks of self-esteem and hope. Hopeful and esteemed individuals are, according to the testimonies we heard in Kabubbu, more likely to become givers and lovers in their own right.

In other words we are told to invest in others as we invest in ourselves and, just as we do not wish to remain dependent on others in perpetuity or to be

---

[35] Cited in Outka 1972: p 64.

[36] Thorne B. (1998). *Person Centred Counselling and Christian Spirituality*. London U.K. Whurr. p 35.

absorbed by others, in acting charitably we do not wish to create a state of dependency or to ensure that recipients end up simply mimicking our behaviour and attitudes, for charity in this one respect is akin to biology in that it seeks to maintain, and enhance, diversity. Diversity is, in the theological sense, a consequence of reverence. Reverence and *agape* directed to the poor, with the intention of increasing their autonomous well-being, are bottom-up processes designed to ensure the survival of the weakest and not just the strongest; another manifestation of the paradox of charity.

The stories in the third part of our pamphlet show how acting charitably fosters responsibility, the manifestation of which is a movement towards independence. The stories stand as contrary evidence to Jeyaraj's suggestion that *'charity is a temporary relief or help rather than an effort to develop self-esteem and justice,'*[37] although, to be fair, he does explain that charity is indeed effective when regarded as a theological and sociological phenomenon. Charity, while being a reactionary and event driven strategy that deals with the consequences of ill-being, does in fact develop self-esteem to a remarkable extent. Our stories also demonstrate that the capacity of an esteemed human being to help others is truly remarkable.

Economically speaking, Christian charity is concerned with releasing value. Christian charity is an act of purposeful investment in the other and for this reason it is Thomas Oord's definition of *agape* that we find particularly useful and practical, for Oord defines *agape* and charity as **'to act intentionally, in sympathetic response to others (including God) to promote well-being.'**[38]

Oord believes that well-being itself can be defined both in terms of its minimum and more advanced levels of attainment. Minimally, well-being is defined as:

---

[37] Jeyaraj J.B. Charity and Stewardship. *ERT,* Volume 28, Issue 2, 2002. p 166.
[38] Oord 2005: 919. Authors' emphasis.

'enhancing mental and physical aspects. It may involve acting to secure sufficient food, clean air and water, adequate clothing and living conditions, personal security, and opportunity. It may involve attaining the satisfaction of being cared for and a sense of belonging...'

At an advanced level, well-being

'may involve acting responsibly to secure a feeling of worth, medical soundness and physical fitness, deep personal relationships, social and political harmony, and the opportunity to develop spiritual/religious sensibilities and practices.'

Further

'acting responsively to increase well-being may involve acting in ways that develop the actor into a person with virtuous dispositions, habits, and character.'[39]

Biographies collected in Kabubbu give testimony to the attainment of both minimal and advanced well-being. The stories stand as testament to the development of 'virtuous dispositions' in recipients. This is how we believe the Samaritan acted. He saw someone in need, someone in an acute state of ill-being, someone not known or close to him, a person that when he got to know him he may not even have liked, yet because he regarded the injured man as a uniquely valuable person he chose to help him. His act of commitment involved the giving of compassion, time and money. The assets under his stewardship flowed in a combined act of spiritual and economic service to the other party. In the jargon of modern economic and business thought the other party to a transaction is frequently regarded as a 'moral hazard'. In other words the assumption is made that the recipient is likely to abuse the assets invested in them, and hence the tendency to impose conditions in the granting of aid. The term 'moral hazard' stresses that the

---

[39] ibid: p 928.

other side to a bargain, transaction or, deal should not be considered trustworthy (although 'we' of course are to be trusted!)

In the economy of Christian charity the reverse is held to be true. Charity is a non-transactional form of economic activity; the wonder of charity is that it transforms without transacting (at least in the conventional, bilateral economic sense of the term)! Giving is an act of confidence underpinned by hope and accompanied by patience. In the economy of Christian charity, confident in our own shortcomings (the log in our own eye), we are asked to regard the beloved as a moral equivalent. Nygren has described *agape* as being an action that is neutral to value, but is nonetheless value creating. In the economy of Christian charity, as we shall see in the second half this book, the consequences of Christian charity are often subtle. In the modern world, we are perhaps conditioned to look only for the obvious and rational, and yet this is not necessarily the environment in which we are called upon to build Kingdom.

So, as we can see, Oord's definition is economic. It calls upon people to act intentionally, to make a strategic choice; to give or not to give. It reminds us that our giving must be underpinned by sympathy (a word he deliberately chooses, which he suggests exceeds empathy). So Oord's definition speaks directly to 1 Corinthians 13 vs. 3:

> 'And though I bestow all my goods to the poor, and although I give my body to be burned, and I have not charity, it profiteth me not.'

The action of giving, without which charity cannot exist, needs to be joined by sympathy or compassion and delivered with humility. Disposal of assets alone is insufficient: emotion alone appears to be equally so. We are called upon to give both spiritually and materially.

Perhaps this is what Lewis meant when he wrote, in The Four Loves,

'William Morris wrote a poem called Love is Enough and someone is said to have reviewed it briefly in the words "It isn't."'[40]

Maybe a similar critique can be levelled at the Beatles' 'All you need is Love.' We need at the highest level to rise above mere emotion and to act purposefully for the benefit of others. We need to understand that the phrase cold as charity is in fact a statement that reflects on rationality, for when our thought processes are spiritual, when a right mind is renewed, a new rationality emerges and it is a rationality that is cold to our own priorities, feelings and natural tendencies. The phrase cold as charity in this light can be regarded as being entirely positive.

Oord's definition also allows us to understand the hoped-for consequences of Christian charity, namely increased well-being. It is important that givers cling onto the word, or virtue, called hope. For hope also forms part of our approach and therefore the economy of charity. If we judge our giving purely on its most obvious consequences we will measure the results of charity according to that which is immediate, obvious and falls within the orbit of our intelligence. We would be trying to measure irrational love with the yardstick of rational calculus: how limiting, how rational.

Well-being is an economic term, subtly different from wealth. Well-being in its minimal form considers basic matters of security - and the Samaritan did this, in making sure that the man he found in the gutter was housed, fed and watered. Christian charity continues to consider others' most basic needs. Donors intermediated by Quicken Trust have for instance built homes, and provided clean water and primary health care, including HIV treatment, for the people of Kabubbu. Well-being on a more advanced level produces self-esteem, income, the growth of intellectual ability, better relationships and finally investment in other vulnerable peoples. Quicken Trust, with its donors, has helped to facilitate advanced well-being by building schools and

---

[40] Cited in Lewis C.S (2002). *The Four Loves, Signature Classics Edition.* London U.K. Harper Collins. p 141.

providing educational sponsorship schemes (there are currently over 400 AIDS orphans receiving primary and secondary education), instigating Alpha courses and establishing community projects. Increased well-being develops both human and social capital for, as our stories show, recipients of gift love invariably become givers themselves; they become agents of *agape*. Wealth, by contrast, tends to be measured purely in relation to the material and financial at the aggregate rather than individual level. Wealth theoretically trickles down. The gains from charity paradoxically trickle, and sometimes flow, upstream.

The promotion of well-being is made possible through acting in reverence. For our hope is that the recipient of charity becomes the person that they were created to be and not the replica or image of ourselves. Gifts given with conditions seek to create the other in our human image; gifts given in genuine Christian charity seek to create the conditions in which the other party can realise their full potential; they become closer to God's image.

Philanthropy is akin to macro or top down investment strategy, whereas Christian charity is a micro discipline. Rowan Williams indicates how John the Dwarf understood the importance of starting from the bottom up. In 'Silence and Honey Cakes' Williams quotes John the Dwarf as stating:

> *'You don't build a house staring with the roof: you start with the foundations.'* And, *'The neighbour is where we start.'*[41]

Starting with our neighbour has the effect of building something rather like a mosaic, a bit at a time, with no obvious overall pattern, and then suddenly, there it is: the overall picture, seemingly unstructured and yet joined together in its beauty, subtlety and, strength. And, it is only *agape*, or charity, that can start with the neighbour (in its redefined sense). Other forms of love are practised within family or friendship groups, whilst the

---

[41] Williams 2003: p 24.

generosity inherent within philanthropy stimulates communal or civic well-being as a first order priority.

We stress that we are not seeking to denigrate philanthropy, which is a good thing, and may even be divinely inspired. But it is not the same as Christian charity. Furthermore, philanthropy may also promote well-being. Indeed it would be very hard to argue that the consequence of genuine acts of philanthropy isn't most frequently an improvement in general well-being, Carnegie's libraries are an obvious example. Christian charity differs from philanthropy in three respects. First, philanthropy tends to be the preserve of the wealthy, whilst charity is the province of the many. Secondly, charity promotes specific well-being as opposed to general or communal well-being. Thirdly, the individual recipient of charity is often then equipped to pass on the baton of charity on their own account.

Christian charity (alongside true altruism and much of philanthropy) responds to a state we might call 'ill-being.' So Christian charity as a virtue, or good, is an antidote to bad or evil and, crucially, it is frequently an intentional act that occurs as we encounter ill-being, or evil. But, as we are reminded in the Parable of the Samaritan, we need to have our eyes (and hearts open), we need to be looking at the world as it really is, rather than designing the world in relation to our business. This willingness to act as we are presented with evidence of ill-being, in the hope that we may help create well-being, characterises Christian charity as an 'event driven' investment strategy which then leads to a long-term commitment, whereby we act intentionally, making free choices as we encounter evidence of ill-being in our daily lives.

Our stories show how the natural consequence of our seemingly non-natural acts of love and investment is an increase in well-being. We hope that our stories all show the consequences of Christian charity as subtle, mosaic like and enduring. The pay-off to the beneficiaries of charitable investment is beyond mere rational calculus. It seems to us that one of the deficiencies in modern thought processes is an over-reliance on proof, verified by mere numbers. We can't provide such proof, but we can give you seventeen stories from the jungle community of Kabubbu that build up a picture. The mosaic is not yet complete; our hope is that others will make the choice to **'to act intentionally, in sympathetic response to others (including God) to promote well-being.'**

In becoming an agent of Christian charity you may feel, like C.S. Lewis, that the actions you choose to undertake undermine your *'congenital preference for safe investments and limited liabilities',* but you can also draw on the same rich well from which Lewis drank that stressed that *'His teaching was never meant to confirm'[42]* our natural tendencies. Christian charity is always accompanied by hope, patience and reverence and it has its own ultimate objective which is, in the words of Lewis, to:

> *'put the recipient in a position where he no longer needs our gift... Thus a heavy task is laid upon this Gift-Love. It must work towards its own abdication. We must aim at making ourselves superfluous.'* **And, humans on the whole don't like to feel superfluous.** *'The hour when we can say they no longer need me should be our reward.'*

However, if

> *'anyone thinks that as a consequence you can stop giving in the meantime, then they have parted company with Christian morality.'[43]*

The stories from Kabubbu testify to the amazing consequences of Christian charity (a sense of responsibility, growing self esteem and, increased well being), but they also tell the story of committed, anonymous givers who kept investing, kept providing and kept loving. To the unnamed, and therefore

---

[42] Lewis C.S (2002). *The Four Loves, Signature Classics Edition.* London U.K. Harper Collins. p 146. Authors' addition and emphasis.
[43] ibid: p 62.

anonymous givers, we and the people we met in Kabubbu, simply say thank you. *Agape*!

Paul Nyakabere (The Halleluiah Man): from parish priest...

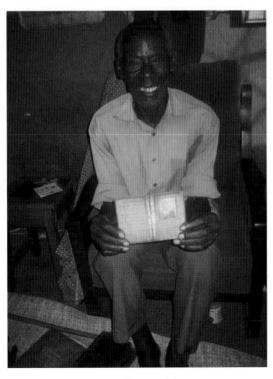

...to village elder

From a shack...

...to a home

...to specialist HIV clinic

From health centre...

From bare subsistence...

...to the dignity of work

SECTION 2

'One's task is not to turn the world upside down, but to do what is necessary at the given place with a due consideration of reality.'
Dietrich Bonhoeffer.

'To get a full sense of the parable of the Good Samaritan we need to use another word: the good asylum seeker, the good Muslim, the good teenager in a hoodie. You have got to get the sense of the unexpected, the despised, that's what the parable is all about.'
Rowan Williams.

Chapter 2
A Reflection on the Story of the Samaritan

Before turning to the true stories of our neighbours in Kabubbu, we make one simple request: that you read one of the most familiar of Jesus' parables and reflect on its implications for you in your environment. When we were discussing the story, we were struck by the fact that the Samaritan, though the archetype of Christian charity, was neither a Christian nor a Jew. Religiosity versus true religion again!

Here is the story in the King James Version:

'And, behold, a certain lawyer stood up, and tempted him, saying, Master, what shall I do to inherit eternal life? He said unto him, What is written in the law? How readest thou? And he answering said:

Thou shalt love the Lord thy God with all thy heart, and with all thy soul, and with all thy strength, and with all thy mind and thy neighbour as thyself.

And he said unto him, Thou hast answered right: this do, and thou shalt live. But he, willing to justify himself, said unto Jesus, And who is my neighbour? And Jesus answering said, A certain man went down from Jerusalem to Jericho, and fell among thieves, which stripped him of his raiment, and wounded him, and departed, leaving him half dead. And by chance there came down a certain priest that way; and when he saw him, he passed by on the other side. And likewise a Levite, when he was at the place, came and looked on him, and passed by on the other side. But a certain Samaritan, as he journeyed, came where he was; and when he saw him, he had compassion on him, and went to him, and bound up his wounds, pouring in oil and wine, and set him on his own beast, and brought him to an inn, and took care of him. And on the morrow when he departed, he took out two pence, and gave them to the host, and said unto him, Take care of him: and whatsoever thou spendest more, when I come again, I will repay thee. Which now of these three, thinkest thou, was neighbour unto him that fell among the thieves? And he said, He that showed mercy on him. Then said Jesus unto him, Go, and do thou likewise.'

For Christians, one of the fundamental motifs of faith is charity. Service, reverence, loyalty, commitment, sympathy, humility, and giving are amongst the essential ingredients which when combined comprise the mosaic we call charity. Benedicta Ward, in The Wisdom of the Desert Fathers recounts the following story:

'A brother questioned an old man, saying there are two brothers. One of them leads a solitary life for six days a week, giving himself much pain. The other serves the sick. Whose work does God accept with greater favour? The old man said: 'Even if the one who withdraws for six days were to hang himself by his nostrils, he could not equal the one who serves the sick.'[44]

We now tell the story of Paul Nyakabere, a story that bears witness to the fact that good grows at compound interest, and that an increase in well-being, sometimes in its minimal, and frequently in its more advanced, forms is the natural consequence of Christian charity. Paul is a remarkable man, a clear beneficiary of Christian charity from a modern day Samaritan.

---

[44] Ward B. (2001). *The Wisdom of the Desert Fathers-4th Impression Edition,* Oxford U.K. SLG.p 61.

Chapter 3:
The Halleluiah Man

We would now like to tell, or rather let him tell you himself, the story of a remarkable man, who was saved from a desperate situation by another remarkable man, whose story we are sadly unable to tell.

The Story of Paul Nyakabere

Paul Nyakabere sits in his mud house under a rusted corrugated iron roof in a chair that is old, though not quite as old as his own eighty-seven years. On the walls of the dark room hang dusty water-stained photographs, faded certificates, a plastic clock that stopped one day at five o'clock, and a picture of a pink-clad Her Majesty Queen Elizabeth II on her visit to Uganda in 2007. On the floor, on rush mats, sit nine of his grandchildren, attention focused on the old man's face. Outside, chickens squawk and scratch, and one wanders untroubled into and around the room. A big red bee buzzes, threatening but harmless, over the children's heads. Suddenly he raises his arms above his head, smiles warmly and shouts, *'Halleluiah!'*

So infectious is the sparkle in his old eyes, so vibrant the tone of his voice, so energetic his movement that it is impossible for any in the room to avoid, or wish to avoid, a full-throated *'Halleluiah'* in response. It is a word that scythes through language barriers, universally recognised by Christians as an expression of joy and praise.

Having seized attention with all the skill of the seasoned preacher, he is able to begin his story.

'I remember little before I left school at the age of twelve. My parents were dead and I went to live in a place called Kabale, where, as I recall, little happened. My adventures didn't really start until after I had set off, at the age of eighteen, with a friend to find work in

Kampala. We didn't get further than Masaka, however, as there was no transport, and we were soon arrested by the police for idleness and disorder. The next thing I knew was that I was sent to a sugar plantation in the East of Uganda for six months' forced labour.

'Within days I developed a serious fever, was sent to hospital for treatment, put straight on the critical list and went into a coma. The medical staff thought I had died and I was sent to the mortuary. It was only when they came to take me for burial that signs of life were detected, and I was returned to the hospital for further investigations and treatment.

'I was there for six months, and as soon as I was discharged I was taken straight back to the plantation, though I was too weak to do much work. After another six months I was released.

'Where should I go? I had no idea. Some of the other ex-prisoners said they were going to Kampala, and asked me to go with them. So I did. Once there we heard of the chance of a job with a rich man near Kabubbu, and got a taxi as far as Gayaza. No sooner had I started the job than again I came down with a fever and couldn't work, so I was dismissed. And my life changed forever.

'Because then I went to work for a man called Nekemeya. He asked my tribe (Mukiga), looked me over and said: 'I want to help you, but you don't have any relatives here. Do you know where the hospital is? Go back to where you are staying and I will get a man to take you to hospital.' So, in some style, I was driven by car to hospital where I was treated well at Nekemeya's expense and eventually discharged.

'Unsure how he would receive me, I reported back for work with Nekemeya. He had no reason to help me, but welcomed me back and astonished me by saying he would look after me until I died. He instructed his wife to look after me as a son, and allowed me to eat with them at the dining table.

'Under the care of this selfless couple I did become in effect their son, and in due course, in the year 1940, they decided it was time for me *to marry. Nekemeya sought to find me a suitable young lady, who turned out to be Ruth who became my lovely wife. On our marriage Nekemeya gave us the land on which my family and I still live, before he himself moved away to Kasawo, where I used to visit him until his death in the 1960s.*

'For all of my life I had been a Catholic, and so it seemed natural that when Ruth gave birth to our first child, a baby girl who died instantly, we should call in the local Catholic priest to bury the infant. But because ours had been a custom marriage, not a Catholic one, he refused to do so and we had to bury the child ourselves.

'Immediately after the burial, and in some quiet anger, I went to see the Usher of the local Church of Uganda and asked to join the Protestant Church, with my wife. We were readily welcomed into the congregation of ten, baptised, attended worship regularly, and I soon became an active and serious church member.

'Eventually, I became an Usher myself and made a commitment to become literate, obtaining my Literacy Certificate on September 20, 1965.'

At this point Paul pauses in his story and with lean and skinny hand, points out the framed document high on the wall and urges a grandchild to reach it down. It comes with a shower of mud from the wall to add to its own carapace of dusty cobweb, but is passed round with reverence and received with due awe.

'Now I could collect and record the offerings in my own right,' Paul continues proudly, 'and my hand, previously always guided by that of the priest, now flowed freely across the record book.' He illustrates with precise waves of his fingers.

'No sooner had I got used to my new role, than the priest, who was also the schoolmaster, unexpectedly left the church and went to look for a new post elsewhere. The congregation had no leader. I immediately went to the Diocesan Vicar to ask for a replacement to

be sent. 'How much money do you collect each week?' was his first and only question. 'Thirty shillings.' 'That's not enough to pay a priest.'

'So the Vicar sent me back, simply telling me that every Sunday I should pray the Our Father, take the collection, and send the congregation home. This I undertook to do, and then the Vicar told me to come to him every Saturday and Thursday for preaching training, which I did with the Vicar in an empty church.

'One day the Vicar gave me a sealed letter to take back to the Chief Usher in Kabubbu, and to spread the word that on the next Sunday the Vicar would be coming to appoint a new priest.

'Sunday came, the Vicar came and the service started. The Vicar stood up, faced the congregation, came over to where I was sitting and seized my hand. He asked me to stand and face the congregation. 'From this day forward,' he stated, 'this is your church Priest.''

Tears fill the corners of Paul's eyes as he recalls this sacred and special moment, and he rummages through envelopes of keepsakes until he finds his appointment card. At the time he entered this post, Paul had five children. But he was given no salary, and later, no pension – about which he has no regrets: *'The One I serve is the one who pays me.'*

Paul ministered to his congregation for many happy years in Kabubbu, but further afield clouds were beginning to gather over Uganda's beautiful land and people. First, a man called Milton Obote forced his way to leadership of the now Republic, only to be overthrown in due course by the brutal Idi Amin, under whose dictatorship the army became a vehicle of fear and repression. No-one knew when the knock at the door would come. For Paul it came one ordinary day in 1979, when he was at home with his family, surrounded by his children (including forty-year old John, now a splendid employee of the Kabubbu Development Project[45]).

'A knock at the door. I didn't need to ask who it was. My heart told me. I refused to answer it. Another knock. Silence. Then bullets began to pummel the back door. Fortunately the internal door was locked. I grabbed my drum and started beating it as hard and loudly as I could. Another bullet, this time holing the inner door, puncturing the kettle and water tank on the living room floor.

'Now I knew. They had come to kill me. I knelt to pray, and as I prayed I heard the soldier shout: 'I have to kill you today, whether you want it or not!' I shouted back, as loud as I could, 'The One I serve will rescue me, and you won't kill me!'

'From prayer I moved to action, took off my shirt and my trousers and in my underwear just managed to squeeze though the small side window, out of sight of both the soldier at the back, and the one who was now at the front. But I was trapped between them. I realised my only hope was to make a dash for the bush, about twenty yards away, hoping that I would reach cover before the front soldier could gather his wits.

'The plan almost worked perfectly. I had just made the edge of the bush when the soldier caught up with me and threw himself on top of me. Summoning, or rather receiving, strength I did not think I had, I wrestled my attacker to the ground from where I managed to throw him off and dive further into the undergrowth. Then I ran and ran, and laid low. Silence. More silence. No one came. Then I knew I had been saved by prayer. But I continued to lie low.

'The next day, my children came to search for my body in the bush. They were sure I had been killed. But when I saw it was them, I

---

[45] Kabubbu Development Project, also referred to as KDP, is a local NGO established by the people of Kabubbu with the support, encouragement and funding of Quicken Trust.

emerged from hiding, embraced them and returned home. The soldiers had moved on. Halleluiah!'

This was not Paul's only encounter with the military. After Amin had been overthrown came the return of Obote, whose 'soldiers' came to the area hunting down suspected members of the National Resistance Movement (NRM). Paul again takes up the story.

'I was on my way to a church fellowship meeting when soldiers invaded the quarry near the church, looking for NRM guerrillas. As I strolled through the forest, a soldier stepped in front of me, blocking my path. At gunpoint he tore off my watch, snatched my church leader's identity card, and then barked: 'Show us the guerrillas!' 'I'm only a priest on my way to church. I've never seen any guerrillas,' I answered with complete truth. My ID card had money in it. 'Take the money, but please leave me the card,' I pleaded. And to my surprise and great relief he relented, pushing the card back into my hand. He ran to catch up with his fellows.

'But that was not the end of it. As I drew near to the church I saw many more soldiers. I was brusquely stopped again. 'Who are you?' 'The priest of this church.' They rummaged through my bag, and appeared convinced by the find of my bible and robes. I was just repeating, 'I don't know where the guerrillas are,' when suddenly the commander, believing he saw movement in the trees, ordered his men to open fire. There were shouts: 'Take cover. There's a man. Kill him!'

'The soldiers started to shoot indiscriminately, and one of the villagers was shot by mistake in the confusion. Every single other person fled the village, leaving me by my church, alone. I had had enough of violence. I just went home.'

This concludes Paul's remarkable story, within which you may find parallels with stories you may have read in another Book. Throughout his years of service and preaching, he says his message to his congregation remained simple and unchanging: accept Jesus Christ.

Forbidden by successive regimes to refer to the government on pain of death, he simply referred his congregation to the 23rd Psalm, and he finds this just as relevant today as ever. Halleluiah!

SECTION 3

Either: *'I do not question the moral duty to help, nor the instinct to want to help the needy, only the form that it takes. On the recipient's side, charity can have devastating effects. It robs the recipient of dignity, and it removes the incentive of having to generate income. It makes the recipient passive and satisfied with thinking all I have to do is sit here with my hand out and I will earn a living.'*
Mohammed Yunus

Or: *'Life is a talent entrusted to us so that we can transform and increase it, making it a gift to others... Each of us belongs to a great family, in which he has his own place and role to play. Selfishness makes people deaf and dumb; love opens eyes and hearts, enabling people to make that original and irreplaceable contribution which, together with the thousands of deeds of so many brothers and sisters, often distant and unknown, converges to form the mosaic of charity which can change the tide of history.'*
Pope John Paul II

Chapter 4:
'In my house there are many mansions'

It is, perhaps, hard for many of us to truly understand what it must be like to live in a tumble down shack on which we are forced to pay rent. How does one feel a sense of dignity in such surroundings, how does one begin to relate to others, how does one invest in the future of our children without the most basic level of security? The stories below all show how the gift of property has been truly transformational in changing desperate lives into more fulfilled and, yes, giving lives.

Peter & Rose's Story

Peter and Rose are the natural parents of Albert. They were married in 1983. Rose was born in Kabubbu; Peter was originally from the west of Africa.

Albert (who has eight siblings, including a baby girl) received the gift of a house in 2008, two days before Christmas. Before that the whole family had lived in a mud house next door, where Peter and Rose still live with their youngest child, whilst their other children occupy the new house, where boys and girls may have different rooms.

Although the change of house has not brought any change of income, Rose is clear that their life overall is much improved.

> *'The problems are still the same, and we still face challenges, but our standard of living is raised. The new house has made a tremendous difference. It was not good before, boys and girls sleeping together in one room.'*

Peter confirms this:

'Our married life has improved. There is less stress. It was uncomfortable living with so many children under one roof. The presence of our children had separated us.'

Peter has a cow, whose milk he used to sell for the benefit of their other children, but it has currently dried up. He also cultivates (as he has always done) the family's own food.

Four of the children are at school. Two have not yet gone to school (not enough money). Two of the older girls refused to go to school because of becoming involved with *'useless, naughty men.'* With obvious pain, Rose expresses her deep concern that the next youngest daughter too will drop out from school.

Peter and Rose are Christians, Rose attending church regularly, Peter far less so. *'I've no time,'* he hurries to explain. Not for the first time, Rose turns away.

Both agree that the gift of the house to Albert has increased Obumu[46] across the family. As Rose puts it:

'It's been like a miracle, something from God. A surprise, just a wonderful surprise. An achievement we never dreamt about. A wonder... I have no words to express it.'

Peter adds:

'Friends say how 'lucky' we are, and ask how we managed to get such 'luck'. We tell them that all this they see is not luck but a miracle from God.'

---

[46] Obumu is a concept which describes a feeling of trust, mutuality, embeddedness in society, and which has some parallels with social capital.

Rose believes that living in peace not war is more important than who leads the country politically. She values peace: *'I am tired of guns.'* She pauses (and it is a long pause) before adding, *'During the war my first baby had to be delivered in the bush, and soon died.'*

The couple now face new challenges: worries about their daughters' moral safety, and in particular (Rose's anguish is visible) that the fourteen year-old may have contracted syphilis; worries about their own health – Peter has a hernia and cannot do the physical work he used to.

But, no longer overwhelmed by the pressure of overcrowding, they now feel more able to confront these obstacles and are determined to do so, the couple's *'wonderful surprise'* of charity now sustained by renewed faith and hope.

Agnes's Story

Agnes was born in Kabubbu some forty years ago.

She welcomes the peace and stability that she believes the present leadership has brought to Uganda, and she has good cause to value such peace. When she was fourteen she had her first baby. Then soldiers came to the village, shooting at random. In the overwhelming panic of the moment she ran for her life, leaving her baby in the house. When she had gone a couple of kilometres, her head cleared, she stopped her flight, realised what she had done, and turned back, ready to fight. *'Now, I was prepared to be killed.'*

Back in the village, she found soldiers everywhere. One challenged her at gunpoint: *'Stop. Where are you going?'*

'To my baby.'

There was a long dreadful silence. The two stared at each other. Something, somehow, made the soldier relent. *'Pick up the baby, and go!'* She escaped, and the child survived, the eldest of her eventual three children, now aged 26, 24 and 21.

Agnes is the aunt of Christine, the recipient of the gift of a house. With them in the house live Agnes's nephew, Sidney, and her youngest daughter, Martha, who has a nine months' old baby, Winston, born after her mother had been *'dumped'* by a man who had *'seized'* her and taken her off to Kampala.

Christine was given the house in January 2009. Previously she, Martha and the others lived in a much more primitive place which Agnes still owns, in the suburbs of Kampala. In practice this two-roomed 'house' is a rowdy pub with a sitting-room bar where Agnes earns a living selling banana beer and kwete (a locally manufactured beer made from millet and maize). Not a place to bring up children: *'There are so many drunkards, and things going on, that the kids in the next room can't sleep or do their homework.'*

Agnes explains how the new house is so much better:

> *'It is bigger and stronger. The kids are away from the drunks. It's also nearer for them to go to school. It's made it possible for me to make the most of my circumstances. I can still make necessary money elsewhere, but I can escape and return to a peaceful environment.'*

She explains the effect on her sense of 'Obumu'.

> *'My situation is very different. I have hope. There was a time when I had even lost the desire to have a nice home, with chairs. Now I feel a challenge and a sense of responsibility, and this has raised my hopes. It is something I never dreamt of. It has made me more ambitious and encouraged me to work.'*

She would like to start a new, different business in Kabubbu.

The change has been spiritual too.

'Before, I believed God had forgotten about me. I left church completely. That was when the roof was leaking and I thought the house was about to fall on us. Now, I'm thankful to God, and at times I think that even if I don't pray God still knows me. But I do pray, and go to church every Sunday.'

Perhaps most of all she values the change in Christine, which she has found to be so remarkable she wonders if it is the same Christine.

'She is no longer rude and resentful. She is more loving and obedient. Not as frustrated with life as she used to be.'

Christine had not wanted to move at first. Much as she disliked the 'pub' she was scared the family would be broken up and that Agnes would not come too. Even when reassured that *'We will go and live there together'* she couldn't believe how it could actually happen. She was old enough to understand family economics, and could not see how they could afford to transport their furniture. She envisaged a series of long, hot burdensome walks. She had reckoned without Quicken Trust.

Godfrey's story

Sixty year old Godfrey was so moved by the gift of a home given to his eight year old son Isaiah by his sponsor that he resolved to work as hard as humanly possible in order to earn enough money to build another home for his other son Eric. Eric, ten, is Isaiah's older brother. The second home is a very basic wood and mud house with a tin roof and stands in contrast to Isaiah's concrete construction, but it is right next door, not twenty yards away, and will be instrumental in keeping the family close and secure in future years. For Godfrey the gift of a home was a strong incentive to work even harder as a woodsman and seller of charcoal. We asked Godfrey how the gift of a home, to his son, had changed him and he replied that it made him *'strong inside.'* This strength led Godfrey to become a giver. Godfrey's story shows that charity does indeed grow at compound interest.

Godfrey's giving is not restricted to his immediate family, for he feels a far greater sense of Obumu now that the family's basic safety needs have been met. Godfrey told us that he *'can do some good to someone else because good was done to him.'* Godfrey does good by lending to his neighbours (he doesn't charge interest). In turn his neighbours have helped Godfrey when he has struggled to generate sufficient income to buy food. Godfrey feels able to interact with his neighbours.

In Godfrey, Isaiah and Eric's old house someone was always ill. When it rained they always got wet, for the old house was grass thatched. When the wind blew they struggled to find warmth. They were obviously poor and they felt impoverished in every way. Godfrey told us that his own health was poor and he looked like a *'hopeless dad'*. Living in such conditions literally sapped the spirit. Godfrey is a devout Christian, yet, for many years he turned away from the church. When he found out that Isaiah was to be given a home the effect was to *'open my eyes and give him faith'*. So Godfrey's life has been transformed spiritually as well as socially. Godfrey and his boys continue to face many challenges. Life is still hard, incredibly so, but with the gift of a home the family at least have a secure base and, with his self esteem much improved, Godfrey lives in hope. Godfrey frequently talks of hope but he also gave other interesting insights that challenge the idea that giving can create dependency for Godfrey revealed that *'the house added a challenge and sense of responsibility'*. Our sense was that Godfrey, for the benefit of his sons, had risen to the challenge of becoming a good and caring father.

Godfrey is a strong man: he has had to be. His wife died eight years ago, just after Isaiah was born. She was ill for two days with a fever and then passed away. Godfrey has brought up his boys single handed. The gift arrived, providentially, shortly after his wife's death. The effect of providence, vested in charity, is surely incalculable. Finally Godfrey's story, like many of the others we tell, provides insights into Oord's suggestion that increased well-being (resulting from Christian charity) can lead to the development of virtuous characteristics and behaviour.

Doreen's story

Doreen is the seventy year old grandmother of homeowner Beatrice. Beatrice is eleven years old and has a younger brother Michael, ten, and their father was one of Doreen's sons. Sadly, he died of AIDS. Doreen's other son is an *'errant father'* and has left his mother with the responsibility of looking after his four year old child. Her son never sees the child and makes no contribution for its upbringing. Doreen's daughter also died of AIDS and she looks after her four year old son. Doreen has had a hard life, her own husband dying just before she came to Kabubbu just over five years ago. At seventy years of age jaaja (the Luganda[47] word for granny) is the family's sole bread winner and carer. Her own health is not good, as she has had two hernia operations, yet she is full of hope.

When Doreen, and her family, first came to Kabubbu they squatted, for a short time, *'in someone else's house'*. Doreen and *'my orphans'* only moved to Kabubbu because they had been evicted from the shack they had erected, on a plot of land owned by the Catholic church in a village six miles from Kabubbu. The church had also refused the family permission to bury their dead on church land: despite this Doreen, a non-Christian, feels no anger or resentment towards the Catholic Church.

Doreen has no doubt in her own mind that she would not still be alive had the sponsor not purchased the land and the property for Beatrice. She also believes that Beatrice and Michael would not be in school where it not for the gift of a home. The home, it seems, has provided the platform from which Doreen can invest in the future well-being of *'my orphans'*.

---

[47] Luganda is the name of the local language

Doreen earns 30,000 UGS[48] per month. She does so from selling a small amount of cash crops, with the majority of her income coming from selling homemade mats. Doreen is also able to grow sufficient crops, in her small garden, to feed the family. Before coming to Kabubbu, Doreen worked as a porter in gardens owned by the Catholic Church. All of the income she made from this was used to buy food for the family. In Kabubbu Doreen is able to grow food to feed the family whilst any surplus can be sold. Her financial situation pre the house was *'just hopeless'*; now she sometimes manages to save a small amount of her income.

The gift given to Beatrice has enabled Doreen to become a better guardian: she has in the dry language of economics, become an investor in human capital. Financially the family are better off as household income seems to have risen. Stocks of social capital have also improved, for Doreen feels a far greater sense of Obumu. Doreen also senses a greater depth to her spirituality: she told us that she felt *'hope and peace'*, she was *'not worried'*, and that the *'house has increased joy and when you have joy you can share joy with neighbours'*.

An act of charity has provided Doreen and her family with dignity, an increased sense of well-being, a platform for growth and joy, all of which Doreen seems determined to share with family and friends, planting small seeds of hope in others. Beatrice was given the house when Doreen was sixty five and consumed by anxiety and fear. At the age of seventy she is a confident, loving and giving jaaja. Charity, as they say, endures.

---

[48] UGS stands for Ugandan Shillings. At the time of the interview UGS10,000 = UK£3

Chapter 5:
'Yea though I walk through the valley of the shadow of death'

The gift of HIV treatment addresses an immediate and obvious medical need. HIV treatment is painful - but worthwhile because it delivers hope: pain is therefore discounted. When hope wins through, fear is the loser. Hope leads the sufferer away from fear and resentment and towards forgiveness. *'Hope is a red hot love story.'* (Kathy Galloway: 'Sharing the Blessing.') Hope is a consequence of true Christian charity.

HIV treatment is a bit like being given a suspended sentence: it holds the condition in abeyance for a 'longish' period. Like all sentences it is passed by another, seemingly dispassionate, person - in this case the carrier.

Nothing is ever the same again for an HIV victim, but, with help (medicine+counselling) life can be 'quickened' and well-being increased.

Treatment benefits not just the immediate recipient but is also a platform for investment in the human capital (potential) of others, specifically their children. As shown in the stories below, each of the women we talked to wanted nothing more than to be a good mother, and father, to their children. With the gift of HIV treatment they are.

Prudence's story

Prudence, fifty-two, is the wife of seventy-two year old Anthony. Prudence brings the family up virtually single handed despite living with her death sentence, for her husband also has HIV. In fact, it was Anthony who gave the disease to his wife of thirty years. Prudence is ashamed of her condition: her pain is palpable and she was keen to stress that she had been faithful throughout her thirty years of marriage. Anthony lives in state of denial, refusing to accept that he is a carrier. The effect of this is that Prudence carries, alone, the full burden of the family's shame. Prudence no longer trusts her neighbours, for she knows that they talk about her and make judgments. She no longer believes in Obumu. She believes in God and, thinks that he has been merciful, but finds it difficult to live alongside her neighbour. She says that people think that she is *'going to befriend their husband',* and so she prefers *'being alone with my family'.*

Prudence has borne the load of looking after the family single-handed for most of her married life. Her husband, a former vet's assistant, retired in 1976. For whatever reason Anthony spent most of the 1980s and 1990s living with his other wife. He returned to the family home with a boy called Edward, who he had fathered whilst 'on sabbatical.' Prudence looks after Edward for her husband. Prudence and Anthony have a thirty-year old son of their own called Arthur. Arthur suffers from epilepsy and is also mentally impaired. Arthur sleeps separately from the rest of the family in a ramshackle building, only partially roofed and with gaping spaces in the walls. His bed has no mattress. Prudence looks after two other children in addition to Edward and Arthur. Life for Prudence is clearly not a bed of roses. Prudence does manage to feed the family, but only one meal a day.

Prudence's medical treatment began in December 2008. We asked Prudence what she believed was the single most significant benefit of her treatment. She told us without treatment she *'would not be able to serve my family'.* She believes that because she has been given the drugs, for which she is clearly grateful, she can be a good mummy. It is truly terrifying to imagine what might become of Arthur in particular were it not for Prudence. Prudence, quite simply, is Arthur's advocate.

When we arrived to talk with Prudence she was about to send Edward to Kabubbu's health centre. Edward looked seriously ill and we asked the boda boda boy (the driver of our scooter-taxi) to take Edward. Edward returned half an hour later. He had been diagnosed suffering from flu-like symptoms, a fungal infection, dehydration, worms and mouth sores, probable evidence of HIV related opportunistic infection.

Prudence cares about Edward despite the fact he is not her son. For Prudence to be a good mother she needs the help of people prepared to stand alongside her in *agape*. Her immediate neighbours either cannot or will not, and for this, amongst other reasons, she needs charity. Edward and Arthur need Prudence and her sole desire is to serve them. When we serve we also give: charity, it seems, quickens service.

Margaret's story

Margaret's story also shows how charity quickens service, but Margaret takes our story one stage further because she shows us how charity also fosters hope. Margaret mothers four children: Susan 9, Joseph 6, Patience 4 and, Maureen 1. As with the many of the women we met, Margaret has no male support; she acts as both mother and father to her family. Margaret has been married twice. Her first husband fathered Susan, her second husband the other three children. Susan's father left Margaret and has now remarried. Her second husband abandoned her.

Margaret was born in Entebbe, some thirty-five miles from Kabubbu, and came to Kabubbu to marry her first husband in 1993. Margaret has worked hard to look after her children, all of whom are clean, tidy and smiley. She works as a porter (casual labourer) in the village, mostly digging, carrying and fetching crops and vegetables. In good times she can earn 90,000 UGS per month from which she can save 20,000 UGS. Her savings are kept under the mattress and used as an emergency fund. Her prudence bears fruit in difficult times such as the 2009 drought. Treatment means that Margaret is able to remain economically active.

Margaret first discovered that she was ill in April 2008. She was seriously poorly for three months prior to her diagnosis. But since receiving the gift of treatment, with the exception of the first two months, she feels *'just like any normal person'*. Like other recipients we spoke to, Margaret reflected on the importance of good counselling in the early stages of treatment. The counsellor provided Margaret with the encouragement to carry on taking the drugs despite the ravaging effect they were having on her body. Margaret told us that good counselling was like having *'God by my side'*. Margaret believes that through the gift of treatment she has *'seen the grace of God'*, incarnated in a person to person relationship. For Margaret was keen for us to understand that had she not been given counselling alongside her drugs she would *'be dead and my children would be orphans in this world, suffering'*. Such is Margaret's love for her children that she kept asserting that she couldn't put into words the gratitude she feels. The best she could articulate was that she could become *'so much a good mother'*. Treatment for HIV in Margaret's case is a platform for motherhood - motherhood is an investment in the well-being of the precious and the vulnerable.

Treatment has without doubt increased Margaret's sense of Obumu, for nowadays *'my house is full of neighbours'*: indeed one of her good friends was present when we met Margaret. Margaret is aware that there is a certain stigma to having HIV, with sufferers frequently seen as perpetrators rather than victims. Margaret chooses to rise above the stigma. Margaret harbours *'no ill feeling'* to her neighbours, her ex-husbands or to the community. Margaret has hope: she and her children have a future.

Charlotte's Story

Charlotte, now 30, came to Kabubbu in 1997, with her first husband, the father of her two oldest children – ten year old Geoffrey, and Esau who is a year younger. At first things went well, and the couple found people willing to lend them gardens to cultivate crops. She was able to sell surplus produce through the local markets, earning around 100,000 UGS a month. Then, in 2002, her husband died of AIDS, and that was only the beginning of Charlotte's troubles.

She had been worried for some time that she too may have been at risk. In 1998 she had given birth to a baby who had died soon afterwards with symptoms of AIDS. However, she herself appeared perfectly healthy until 2005 when she started to experience bouts of nausea. In fear, she delayed seeking diagnosis or treatment, and it was a whole year before she plucked up the courage to seek professional medical help.

The fear she had experienced was reinforced by the diagnosis of HIV. On the way to and from the hospital in Kampala she kept imagining how she might die, and wondering what would become of her still young boys.

She was given drugs and told not to worry. But at first she experienced bad side-effects from the regime and felt even worse. She was tempted to give up the treatment altogether, until a counsellor who came to see her at home persuaded her to stick with it, and eventually her body started to adjust and the drugs began to work.

This successful outcome has enabled her to cope with the discomfort that the drugs continue to cause her.

> *'I still have to be examined regularly – a problem as I don't have transport – and I can't say that I feel well yet. But I do feel better physically.*

> *'The bad feeling inside me has come back recently, though. It's a spiritual thing, not a physical thing.'*

This depressed feeling has been accentuated by her financial difficulties, and that fact that all her relatives live many miles away in Entebbe. To cap it all, she has not experienced Obumu from her neighbours.

> *'After my husband's death I was turned out and chased from his family. The people nearby were all friends of my late husband, and so I'm looked down on. They treat you like you were a stranger, and not a normal human being. My children are stigmatised by other children.'*

HIV victims, it seems, are seldom treated with reverence, respect, or sympathy by their immediate neighbours. This is why they benefit from the type of love inherent in charity.

From somewhere within her Charlotte is able to forgive them all, but has become the stranger they want her to be. *'I now simply stay away from them, and that's where I find peace.'* Spurned by these humans, she has drawn closer to God. As she puts it: *'When I received the help of treatment I knew God was assisting me. God has done what I did not expect.'*

Although she eventually found another partner, who fathered her beautiful nine month old baby, Godfrey, he soon left the scene and is now *'far away'*. Then, the owner of the borrowed land she had continued to cultivate sold up, so the means of supporting her family vanished overnight. This has further shaken her confidence and she struggles, not always successfully, to maintain a positive hold on life.

From Charlotte's isolation come some rays of hope. She firmly believes that the gift of the drugs has enabled her to continue to be the loving mother her children need and so nearly lost. And she is beginning to contemplate how she might return to work some day.

Ruth's Story

Nine people sleep in Ruth's small but organised and tidy house. She is forty, and the proud mother of eight children. Her first-born, Christine, was the product of the union with her first partner, who was killed in an accident. Ruth is justly proud of Christine's achievements at school, and keeps her reports and certificates close at hand.

Agnes (17), Peter (15), Hannah (14), Patience (12), Simon (10), Andrew (9) and Percy (7) all come from her marriage to her second husband, who died on August 5, 2007, only three months after his diagnosis with HIV/AIDS.

After his death Ruth had to bring in an income. She started crushing stones in the quarry, earning 50,000 UGS a month (*'when I wasn't cheated by the lorry drivers'*), just enough to provide her children with one meal a day, plus the occasional bar of soap for the house and some school fees. But now her chest is painful after physical exertion and she has had to give up quarry work. She still manages to cultivate some food herself – the hoe stands at the ready in her doorway – but the recent drought has been devastating and the family has had to make do with boiled cassava roots, supplemented for a time by a welcome gift from a sponsor of a bag of milled maize.

Late in 2007 she began to feel unwell, and when her husband died she was frightened and sensibly sought an immediate HIV test. *'When I was told I was positive I got such a shock. I went home and looked at the children and started crying. I cried every day'.*

Treatment started immediately, with Ruth desperate to get back to her children. At first she had to travel a long distance to the Kasangati Centre but now it is much more conveniently available in Kabubbu itself at the Trust clinic.

Now that her condition is being managed, Ruth looks back wryly on her late husband's behaviour.

> *'He had other 'wives' – one in every trading centre! - whom he tried to keep secret. I knew all about it, though, including that he had had a child by another woman. At first it hurt, but then I just got used to it,'*

she adds phlegmatically.

The effects of the drugs hurt too at first:

> *'I felt like vomiting all the time. But my counsellor told me to make sure I took the tablets with food, especially protein. And bit by bit my body got stronger as it got used to the drugs. Now I feel joy, because*

before I was sure I was just going to die with the sickness and the shivering. Yes, now it is joy.'

The experience has made a huge impact on Ruth's life. First because she *'developed hope in God'*, and secondly because with her counsellor's help she has learned that the best way to deal with her situation is to engage actively with other people, so she forgets her own troubles. Her sense of Obumu has been consolidated, not least by not allowing herself to be stigmatised.

'I didn't mind what other people said. I ignored their gossip, and instead tried to take a real interest in them as people.'

Her self-esteem (advanced well-being) has been boosted.

This approach has paid off in several ways. She has a supportive circle of friends, and a close prayer partner, whose support has been crucial. Her late husband's family (who knew all too well about his wayward habits) have also been supportive and even offered to help look after one child. Her mother-in-law sometimes brings gifts of food.

Coming back from the brink of death through the gift of medical treatment leading to prolonged life expectancy has, she says, helped her to be an even better mother (and father too) to her children. Every responsibility is upon her shoulders alone. In particular she has to think carefully about how to bring up her boys to be responsible. There are so many temptations and distractions out there, including card schools and alcohol. She emphasises to them how much HIV there is in the community. She is proud of her parenting so far, and her children show self-discipline, which deeply pleases her.

Chapter 6:
'When seed falls on good soil'

Just as in the parable of the sower (Matthew 13, 1-9) we discovered a multiplier effect when gifts given are put to good effect. Maybe this is what C.S. Lewis had in mind when he reflected that good grows at compound interest. In all of the following four stories we see how the gift of an economic asset leads to a significant increase in income. We were delighted to hear how such gifts also led to self-esteem, personal growth, the desire and ability to act as a good neighbour, and to be seen as a role model and specialist in the local community.

Cuthbert's Story

Cuthbert is a young looking 63 year old from a nearby village who came to Kabubbu in 1978 to work in a nearby government project. He and his wife Lily had three children before she died in 2003, believing herself to have been *'bewitched'* (though Cuthbert more pragmatically suspects a stomach tumour). He has not found anyone to replace her, and has willingly taken on the role of bringing up Teddy (15), Verity (10) and Peter (8).

The family now live in the house gifted to Teddy in 2004, a huge improvement on their previous grass construction. Cuthbert now scratches a living as a casual porter (when there is work). He does not count up any money he earns from this labour because it is spent as soon as it is earned on food: *'Whatever I get, we eat.'* In good weather (that is when there is no drought as at present) bought food is supplemented by what he can cultivate around the property.

Cuthbert also looks after the pigs gifted to Teddy. Originally there were four but two quickly died. The other two, however, were successfully fattened and sold for 100,000 UGS each.

He used this income first to pay school fees, and then to reinvest in the business by buying two pigs (males, because cheaper – a two month-old female costs 20,000 UGS). These are now being fattened for nine months, after which they too will be sold for 100,000 UGS apiece.

Once they are mature enough he will be able to rent the boars out to other village pig-keepers for insemination at 500 UGS for each sow served. In theory this could be on a daily basis, and although this rate may be difficult to achieve in practice, Cuthbert believes that this part of the pig business could bring in some 15,000 UGS in a good month.

Just as much as the financial benefit, the pigs have brought Cuthbert a new sense of purpose and self-respect.

> *'I've become a specialist, and people come to me for help. One man has even lent me a pig to raise for him, and when this is sold I will be given half any piglets.*
>
> *'Looking after the pigs gives me a sense of joy, and many of the neighbours help and give me grass for the pigs: they see them as theirs as well as mine. And in return I can now be of some use to my neighbours. For example, I can buy maize with my income and make porsha which I can share for free with the neighbours, as a thank-you for the grass and grazing.*
>
> *'All the children get involved too with looking after the pigs, which is good since the income is for the whole family. It is a blessing.'*

As an illustration of how the gift of a physical asset can multiply 'a thousand fold' by the growth of responsibility, self-respect and love for others Cuthbert's story could hardly be bettered.

Prosy's Story

Prosy, a vigorous 58 year-old, came in 1980 from a small town 20 kilometres away to marry her husband Isaac. They had five children, two of whom (Mary, 15, and Elizabeth, 13) still live with her in the house gifted to Elizabeth in 2004.

Isaac died an untimely and distressing death from a fever many years ago, but Prosy also shares the house with six grandchildren, the offspring of the couple's older children who, for one reason or another, are unable to raise them themselves – though they may make occasional small financial contributions.

> *'When Isaac died, I was alone. He was my only friend in life. I had no brothers or sisters and was away from my home village.'*

Isolated but undaunted, Prosy provided for her family by cultivating food on 'common' land, land which subsequently was taken back by the owners, leaving her without the means to grow any crops. She had no other income. Hope came when she was able to move into the new house with Elizabeth, Mary and an expanding number of grandchildren. A year ago came a further gift, this time of chickens which it fell to Prosy to look after. It is no exaggeration to say that this has transformed her, and her family's, life.

The initial gift was of a hen-house and thirty chickens. A further fifty arrived later in the year. Although inexperienced and untrained, she was a fast learner and has tended the chickens with great care and increasing expertise. At the time of writing she is preparing to separate the original thirty for sale for food, as they have recently become off-layers. These should fetch about 150,000 UGS, enabling her reinvest in the business to buy immunised replacement chicks. (She hopes to be trained to do her own immunisation in the future.)

Income from sale of eggs has been approximately 4,000 UGS per day from the first 30 birds, and 5,000 UGS per two days from the second 50 (who have not yet reached full laying power). In total, some 100,000 UGS a month.

Her (realistic) dream now is to become, like Cuthbert, a specialist, a local expert to whom others will turn for advice. And beyond this new sense of ambition and the positive change in family income, the arrival of the chickens has been transformational in Prosy's life.

Prosy now actively and regularly interacts with her neighbours, partly for good business reasons and partly just because she wants to. Examples abound of how this has led to mutual giving, such as when she gives eggs for church fundraising or local festivities.

Eloquently and simply she says:

> *'Without the gift I am not sure that I would now be alive with my family.*
>
> *'A mother always feels happy and becomes a good mother when she has something to give to her family, especially when she is recovering from a situation when there was nothing at all to put on the table. What has happened has eased my loneliness and I now feel very self-sustaining. It has helped remove that feeling of losing a friend and having to stand alone.'*

Jean's story

Fifty nine year old Jean was born in Kabubbu. Her husband left Jean five years ago. Initially she was in desperate straits as she was left to bring up her four children all by herself. Subsequently Jean has taken into her care her four grandchildren, whilst her two daughters Hannah and Sarah have moved on with their lives. Jean explains that *'they have left home but not married'*. For most of the last five years Jean has struggled to house, care for and educate a total of eight children. She did so by working as a porter. A porter's income is variable, and in a drought a porter's income diminishes rapidly: in good times a porter can earn 50,000 UGS per month. In Jean's case that is just over £17 per month to feed and clothe a family of nine. There is no status or esteem in being a porter.

In June 2008 Jean was provided with a home. Previously Jean had lived in a small house left to her by her late father. Jean and her extended family were chased out of her home by her brothers and sisters. Jean explained to us that they were in reality only her half siblings: her father it seemed had conceived her with another woman. The house provided Jean and her family with security, but on 25th May 2009 Jean received an additional gift, ninety chickens. We asked Jean how she felt on receiving the household gifts and, she replied *'too much happiness'* and, *'deep down in my heart very grateful'*. *'I thank God for a relationship with people in the U.K. I have never seen'*.

It is too early to quantify precisely how much economic difference the chickens will make but Jean believes that she will be able to sell sufficient eggs to generate an additional 100,000 UGS per month. Jean feels that the gifts are a responsibility. She says that the *'gift is the beginning for being responsible for my family's well-being'*.

Jean is not used to being held in esteem in the local community, so the fact that her neighbours now look up to her and come to her for advice on rearing their own chickens fills her with joy. Jean gets *'joy when I teach them'*. Jean is in no doubt that she is able to assist others because of the training she herself received. The gift of chickens, her hope for the future and, the training she received boosts her Obumu.

Jean continues working as a porter and needs to do so until the chickens hatch. We asked Jean whether she considers herself to be a porter or a keeper of chickens. Quick as flash, and with a broad grin, Jean told us that she is *'a poultry farmer'*. The gift given to Jean certainly seems to have landed on fertile ground. The growth process has begun.

Edith's story

Edith, 43, is a tailor. Edith's story differs from the others told because she works not alone, but in a group. Edith, in fact, heads up the village tailoring group of which there are currently three active members. The tailoring group was established in 1999, and prior to its formation Edith had worked alone. As a sole trader Edith earned 14,000 UGS per month. The paucity of her earnings meant that she frequently defaulted on the children's school fees. Her children dropped out of school for two years. Edith is proud that her first born, Kenneth, has now finished school and is undertaking a vocational course at a technical school. As the leader of the tailoring group Edith earns over 100,000 UGS per month. The other members of the group earn 50,000 UGS per month. We asked Edith how much a sewing machine, such as the model they use, would cost. *'200,000 shillings,'* was the reply. Four months wages would therefore be consumed in repaying the cost of equipment required to work as a tailor in Kabubbu, assuming an interest free loan. Interest free loans tend not be on offer in the commercial money markets!

Edith, as leader of the group, is responsible for teaching the other members. She takes her responsibility seriously. The group meet every afternoon to sew, the mornings being spent working in their gardens growing subsistence crops. Edith is convinced that the group structure works. She told us that *'you can't earn money when working individually.'* We didn't understand why this should be so. It appears that the answer lies in peer group pressure. Each member of the group encourages the other even when they are tired. Group members are effectively paid a piece rate, with their earnings being dependent on garments completed. Until recently there were six members of the group. One died and two have chosen to cease tailoring and look after their animals instead. Edith is open to the leavers rejoining the group if they are unsuccessful in their new ventures.

Edith was initially sceptical about group work, but now she would have it no other way. She believes *'you can't establish a business without Obumu'.* The resulting increase in earnings has allowed her to diversify: she now keeps a pig. Edith has also been able to build an additional two rooms onto the home that she was given. This means that the ten boys and girls under her care (six children of her own and four orphans) can now sleep in single sex rooms. Her economic success, vested in an initial gift, has allowed her to diversify and invest in the potential of the next generation.

Edith is in no doubt that the gifts she has received have been a catalyst for growth for, within a few minutes of meeting us, she proclaimed that *'before gifts I was a nobody'.* By the end of our discussion we were convinced that the nobody had become a somebody.

Chapter 7:
'When I needed a neighbour'

The following stories are about people in vulnerable or even dangerous situations who received gifts of counselling, personal support, prayer or all three. They demonstrate that love given can beget love in others, and also promote practical giving. Common themes are increased hope and strength. We found it interesting that those with least hope and most fear had no home to call their own.

It underlined to us once again how powerful the role of the counsellor can be. As Brian Thorne, Emeritus Professor of Counselling at the University of East Anglia, has observed:

'Jesus was both a great lover and greatly loved. It is my experience that those who have found healing through a relationship with a counsellor always discover that they, too, are loveable and capable of loving.'[49]

Beatrice's story

Twenty four year old Beatrice told us: *'It is hard for me to understand; I have no hope'.* Yet Beatrice has friends in her counsellor and prayer partner and a close neighbour, Irene, whose friendship she cherishes and who she desires to help. Irene is apparently *'a good lady with good manners, but needy; she has five children'.* Beatrice's story is tragic, and it is easy to understand why she feels hopeless, yet she also has undoubted strength.

Beatrice shares a house with five others. The house is owned by her husband Gerald, thirty-four. Gerald and Beatrice have a one-year old daughter, Alexandria. Beatrice is pregnant. Beatrice has two children from her marriage

---

[49] Thorne 1998: p 35.

to Francis, Peter who is seven and Horatio who is six. Francis died in 2006 of a liver condition. Beatrice was very much in love with Francis: she described him as 'so, so good'. The contrast between her first and current marriage moved Beatrice to tears.

Gerald refuses to acknowledge or take any responsibility for Peter and Horatio. He is only prepared to spend money on their daughter, Alexandria. She is only allowed to feed the elder children because of the effort she puts into cultivating the gardens they rent. *'I have to do it all alone'*, she explains. Beatrice is scared of Gerald: she told us, *'I have so many reasons why I fear him'*. Gerald was *'rude and careless'*. Gerald's behaviour to Beatrice left her feeling useless, without strength and ill equipped to mother her children. When Beatrice was at her lowest ebb she turned to her counsellor for support. She has spent time with Beatrice supporting her with prayer and practical advice. Beatrice still feels hopeless but she also says she has been strengthened. Before the counselling began Beatrice thought she *'was going mad'*. Beatrice is clearly not mad; sad yes, but not mad. Beneath the despair there is strength and clarity. She has reached a place of resolution, 'I *know I will not manage in this marriage. I am here temporarily. I will leave'*, she told us. Without the support of a good neighbour it is likely that Beatrice would have cracked. Support has led Beatrice to a place where she knows what she ultimately needs to do for the good of her children.

Although Beatrice has lost her much loved husband and been berated, neglected and hurt in her present marriage, she retains the capacity to care. She wishes to give to her children and her friends. We gave Beatrice 20,000 UGS: she was going to use half of it to buy food for herself and the children (her husband apparently eats elsewhere) and use the other half to help her friend Irene. When her neighbour needs her, she will be there.

Maureen's story

Maureen, fifty, was born in Kabubbu. Maureen currently lives alone, and in considerable fear. Her second husband, Anthony died of AIDS just over a year ago and, Maureen knows that she is going to be chased out of 'their' home. Maureen is to be evicted because local custom dictates that because she bore no children during their marriage, the house, barely a shack, becomes the property of the eldest son from Anthony's previous marriage. It seems that the only legacy that Maureen will take from her marriage is HIV, from which she now suffers. Maureen was only married to Anthony for four years. She had ten children from her first marriage to Richard who died in 1987. Seven of her children died; intriguingly the other three now live in Canada. Maureen is all alone.

When Maureen is evicted she will return to the place where her parents lived and throw herself on the mercy of her brothers. She hopes that they will give her a room to sleep in. They certainly won't be able to provide her with a small plot of land on which to grow crops and vegetables. Maureen needs to work as she can't subsist.

For the last year Maureen has worked in the Kabubbu Development Project gardens. Augustine, a project leader, whom Maureen calls 'daddy', gave her the job. Previously Maureen worked in the quarry smashing stones. Maureen earns 60,000 UGS per month and from her earnings she is always sure to buy meat, soap and sugar for her auntie. Augustine is not just her employer, he is also her friend. He talks to her nicely and this makes her happy. Augustine encourages Maureen to help her friends. Consider if you will the importance of kindness, a generous smile and a tender voice. Contrast this with the loneliness of home where Maureen sits waiting for the savage and triumphant entrance of her evictor. Maureen has asked Augustine to help her find a new home and he has promised to do his best. Maureen believes meeting Augustine has changed her life. We asked her how and her reply was breathtaking in its simplicity. She said *'with kindness in his eyes and help from his pocket, why would life be the same?'* Has Maureen, perhaps, defined Christian charity?

Faith's Story

Faith (32) was born in the next village and only came to Kabubbu in 2000 when she married her husband Charles, a man well thought of as a builder in a neighbouring town. She has two children of her own (Julian, 8 and Allan 4), and two (Marjory, 9 and Susan, 14) from her husband's previous wife whom he had left.

Charles' business brings in a reasonable income, sufficient at least for food and school fees and Faith has no need to work. The family home is adequately furnished, and has comfortable seating and a television. On the surface, things appear to be going well.

In 2006, however, around the time of Allan's birth, Faith began to be troubled because of her husband's relationship with other women. This concern grew into serious inner turmoil:

'I was in deep sorrow because of his behaviour, and I developed a hunger in my spirit for help, and I didn't know where to go.'

Although Faith came from a secular family, the first person who offered Faith help happened to be the wife of a Christian minister and it was through her that she met a Christian counsellor from the Kabubbu Development Project.

'She was such a kind lady and interested in my baby and played with her, and it was through this that I started to get to know her.'

The counsellor talked to Faith and gave her moral support in her sadness and troubled mind, and at times prayed for her. She found herself strengthened by this and gradually became convinced that she wanted to follow a Christian path in life. She began to pray to Christ herself, experienced a sense of personal relationship, and felt a difference in the way she felt about herself and her problems.

Because of her husband's scorn of religion, Faith has had no option but to keep her new faith secret within her heart, bravely attending Christian worship outside the village. She is also taking her own children to a Christian nursery, again at considerable risk, since she cannot predict (or probably can) her husband's reaction to her coming to faith.

When going to church is too much of a risk, she tunes in to services on a Christian radio station. Although the conversion to Christianity was her choice, made freely and autonomously, she is deeply grateful to her counsellor for her support. Faith says that before, she carried all her problems around all day in her head, but now they are substantially lifted, although she recognises that they have not all gone away.

> *'I feel better, and a better mother, because now I can give my problems to God, and when I do that the problem is lifted.'*

This feeling has given her strong hope that she will continue to progress:

> *'If God helps me I cannot fail, now or in the future. My best prayer, one I learned from a close friend, is to have faith in God, and trust in him fully.'*

Obumo has not been easy. In her deepest depression she thought her friends were not useful to her, so she abandoned them. Through her prayer partner she has now made new friends, and to these she gives back her heart and her love. In concrete terms she does this through practical giving to people with needs, perhaps a dress or other article of clothing. Even, once, a cow. While we were with her a friend came to her door to ask for help: further evidence if it were needed that love begets love.

Joyce's Story

Born in Kabubbu, and married to a woodcutter, Joyce (28) is a woman who has a problem with men. Two in particular: her husband, and her landlord.

Her husband, the father of the couple's four children (Roy, Hatty, Eugenie and Ruth – who range from 12 to 3) earns some 100,000 UGS a month, but he only gives her 1,000 UGS a day for food or 5p per person. He himself usually eats elsewhere (cost unknown). Rent is 18,000 UGS per month, and school fees a further 40,000 UGS a month. Such financial pressure has led to the second problem.

Currently the couple owe the landlord 60,000 UGS, with no apparent prospect of payment. Joyce explains,

> *'The landlord has started getting angry, and he calls round at night when I am on my own, shouting and frightening me. My husband is never in. I don't know where he is – down in the trading centre I think, chatting to friends. Now whenever I see the landlord my heart jumps, and I picture him coming and humiliating me in front of the neighbours.*

> *'When my husband comes back and I tell him, he just says 'We will pay him tomorrow' and the next day it is the same, and the next. He isn't caring. He doesn't tell me the truth, even with money. He has no truth in him.'*

Things reached breaking point for Joyce five months ago, and she had made up her mind to abandon her husband and her children, pack her bag, and go back to her parents. Then, after a visit to her local church, with one final act of will she decided to go down to the house of the Director of the Kabubbu Development Project and throw herself on his mercy. At that stage she could not even speak. All she could do was cry. She was beyond coping.

It was again a counsellor who gathered her up, prayed for her, and began to provide nurturing support.

> *'Her prayers and encouragement were so helpful. They made me feel strong, and gave me the ability to resist.'*

In particular, she found reading and reflecting on the story of Job gave her strength and consolation. She does not yet feel free from her distress, but acknowledges she has made progress, perhaps reaching a half-way point, an equilibrium which could next tip either way.

Although she has problems she has hope, and she is learning to re-find Obumo in the interaction with her friends. She now knows who her good friends are, as well as those who might mislead. Many of her former 'friends' just advised her to abandon her children.

At times she still feels very low. Particularly when she and her children sit down, without husband or father, to their one daily meal of potatoes, cassava or groundnut soup. Continuing support will be important in the coming months.

Conclusion

'Religion that God our Father accepts as pure and acceptable is this: to look after the widows and orphans in their distress and keep oneself from being polluted by the world.'[50]

In our researching for this pamphlet we sought information from three sources: the stories told to us in the field, or should we say the jungle, by some very grateful recipients of Christian charity, academic literature and scripture. We have been involved in an exercise that may be regarded as one of practical theology, in other words theology grounded in experience with real world socio economic implications. The academic literature provided us with a specific definition of *agape* or Christian charity, Oord's definition, which describes *agape* as **'to act intentionally in sympathetic response to others, to promote well-being.'** The definition can, in our view, be clearly validated through scripture (The Parable of the Samaritan) and also through the stories we have been able to tell. We hope that we have demonstrated that, far from leading to dependency, true Christian charity leads to responsibility. It does so quietly for the majority of donors are anonymous to all but the recipients of their gift-love, and to Quicken Trust. The tendency towards responsibility also results from the ethical underpinning that accompanies *agape*, reverence and commitment. Reverence, commitment, anonymity, intentionality, hope, selfless giving and love are the specific attributes that combine to effect Christian charity. Is it any real surprise that responsibility and well-being are the likely outcomes? Christian charity offers, from the ground upwards, the very real possibility for transformation and stands contrary to other transactionally orientated approaches. Christian charity is concerned exclusively with the interests of the other, or the beloved, and despite criticism from the cynics, it seems to effect deep and meaningful change. Christian charity is a good that when invested in the beloved other grows at compound interest.

---

[50] James 1 21 New International Version

Afterword

The journey we have been on has led us to a destination where we can say, with confidence, that charity speaks to the poor, afflicted, destitute, hopeless, trampled and abused. It speaks with clarity because the words uttered quietly to the beleaguered are met with gratitude, and because the recipient knows, sometimes for the first time, that they are both respected and loved. Christian charity speaks clearly because it is quickened by intent and consummated in action. Christian charity is directed towards our neighbour. Who is he? Anyman and Everyman. Our encouragement is this: go and speak clearly to your neighbour. *Agape*.

Bibliography

Books

Eagleton T. (2007). *The Meaning of Life.* Oxford U.K. Oxford University Press.

Eagleton T (2009). *Reason, Faith and Revolution.* U.K. Yale University Press.

Foster R. (2004). *Streams of Living Water; celebrating the great traditions of the Christian Faith.* Westbury U.K. Eagle.

Galloway K. (2008). *Sharing the Blessing; Overcoming Poverty and Working for Justice.* London U.K. SPCK.

Glover J. (1999). *Humanity – a Moral History of the Twentieth Century.* London U.K. Jonathan Cape.

Gold L. (2004). *The Sharing Economy.* Aldershot U.K. and Burlington U.S.A. Ashgate.

John Paul II (1998). *In my own words.* London U.K. Hodder and Stoughton.

Lewis C.S. (2002). *Mere Christianity 50th anniversary edition.* London U.K. Harper Collins.

Lewis C.S (2002). *The Four Loves, Signature Classics Edition.* London U.K. Harper Collins.

McGrath A. (1999). *Christian Spirituality.* Oxford U.K. Blackwell.

Nygren A. (1953). *Agape and Eros (translated by Phillip S. Watson, in 1969).* New York U.S.A. Harper Torchbooks.

Outka G. (1972). *Agape and Ethical Analysis.* New Haven U.S.A. Yale University Press.

Peck S. (1990). *The Road Less Travelled.* London U.K. Arrow.

Phillips K. and Taylor B. (2009). *On Kindness.* London U.K. Hamish Hamilton.

Polkinghorne J. and Beale N. (2009). *Questions of Truth.* U.K. Westminster John Knox Press.

Ridley M. (1997). *The Origins of Virtue.* U.K. Penguin.

Sacks J. (2003). *The Dignity of Difference.* New York U.S.A. Continuum.

Schumacher E. (1977). *A Guide for the Perplexed.* U.K. Sphere Books.

Soble A. (1989). *Eros, Agape and Philia-Readings in the Philosophy of Love.* New York U.S.A. Paragon House.

Thorne B. (1998). *Person Centred Counselling and Christian Spirituality.* London U.K. Whurr.

Ward B. (2001). *The Wisdom of the Desert Fathers-4th impression edition,* Oxford U.K. SLG.

Williams R. (2003). *Silence and Honey Cakes-The Wisdom of the Desert.* Oxford, U.K. Lion.

Yunus M. (1999). *Banker to the Poor.* London UK. Aurum.

Journals

Bonner M. (2005). Poverty and Economics in the Qur'an. *Journal of Interdisciplinary History,* xxxv: 3, Winter, pp 391-406.

Burns P.E. (2006). Altruism In Nature As Manifestation Of Divine Energeia, *Zygon,* Volume 41, No.1. March, pp 125-137.

Cole D. (1999). Thomas Aquinas on Virtuous Warfare, *Journal of Religious Ethics,* Volume 27, Issue 1, Spring, pp 57-80.

Dulles A. (2007). Love, the Pope and C.S. Lewis. *Monthly Journal of Religion and Public Life,* Issue 169, January, pp 20-24.

Edwards M. and Sen G. (2000). NGO's, social change and the transformation of human relationships: a 21st Century civic agenda, *Third World Quarterly,* Volume 21, No.4, pp 605-616.

Grant C. (1996). For Love of God. *Journal of Religious,* Volume 24, Issue 1, Spring, pp 3-19.

Jeyaraj J.B. (2004). Charity and Stewardship. *ERT,* Volume 28, Issue 2, pp 166-173.

Judish J. (1998). Balancing Special Obligations with the Ideal of Agape. *Journal of Religious Ethics,* Volume 26, Issue 1, pp 17-45.

McCloskey D. (2004). Capital Gains-How economic growth benefits the world. *Christian Century,* May, pp 24-30.

Oord T.J. (2005). The Love Racket: Defining Love and Agape for the Love-and-Science Research Programme. *Zygon,* Vol. 40, No. 4, December, pp 919-938.

Watts R. E. (1992). Biblical Agape as a Model of Social Interest. *Individual Psychology,* Volume 48, Number 1, March, pp 35-40.